# Th Power of God in a Testimony

## *A Memoir of Short Stories and Testimonies*

# Barbara Jeanette Shephard

Foreword: Bishop Johnny A. Tates

ISBN 978-1-63874-308-8 (paperback)
ISBN 978-1-63874-309-5 (digital)

Christian Faith Publishing, Inc.
832 Park Avenue
Meadville, PA 16335
www.christianfaithpublishing.com

Scripture quotations are taken from the *Holy Bible* King James Version, public domain.

Printed in the United States of America

Barbara is a living witness to what faith in God really means (Hebrews 11:1). This book is a great read for individuals going through a trial and/or preparation for future trials. I am grateful to God for allowing our paths to cross on this journey of life.

—Evelyn K. Chambers

How great is our God! In the pages of *The Power of God in a Testimony*, Barbara has showcased the wonder and love of God, page after page, testimony after testimony! This easy-to-read account from Barbara will encourage and inspire you, leaving you with a strengthened resolve to follow her example of unapologetic praise!

—Cheryl Hulett

What a God-given testimony from birth until now. In the thirty-eight-plus years I have known her, I have seen her trust in God and her walk of faith. To God be the glory for the things he has done for her. Praise the Lord.

—Sandra Williams

Barbara's masterpiece of artwork reflects strong faith, humility, and deep compassion while enduring tumultuous advertise to be able to push with her million-dollar smile.

I am genuinely impressed with Barbara's ability to endure the pain knowing that when God permits his children to go through the furnace, he keeps his eye on the clock and his hand on the thermostat.

This woman of God has demonstrated long-suffering with some peace, a quiet spirit, sense of humor, whereby many would have begrudged the trials/tribulations of dialysis and chemotherapy every other day. But OMG, her manuscript displays resilience every time she was hospitalized/having many surgeries followed by endless medications.

This work of art is truly a masterpiece because this lady has been able to endure pain and suffering while ultimately encouraging her family and others to forge ahead beyond any obstacles. This Christian lady has been victorious as a prayer warrior, who has survived multiple crises in her life and yet maintain sound decisions to motivate and encourage her family and others.

—Lorna Harrison

I call this book "The Book of Faith." After all of the of the adversities that she has gone through, she continues to give God the praise. She has never become bitter. She was met with a challenge and God gave her the strength and courage to go through. She reminds me of the "energizer battery" that keeps going, going, and never give up.

—Hersey Matthews

Barbara's life story is the epitome of a trooper indeed. This book will literally walk you through her numerous walls encountered and the victories won. Her journey is a testament of *"For by thee I have run through a troop; and by my God have I leaped over a wall"* (Psalms 18:29). She continually gives God glory and remains confident of his promise to be with her always, even during the last leap.

—Mildred J. Shephard

To the most loving, wonderful, kindest, God-fearing people in my life: my father, mother, and sister, the late Jesse C. Shephard, the late Aslee Pasalee Alabama Tennessee Shinick-Shephard, and the late Dr. Sealy Marie Shephard-Pollard. Until we meet again. Take your rest, Mother, Daddy, and Sealy!

In memory of my niece, Laurie Helaine Shephard, and my nephew, Jermaine Shephard. You are truly missed by loved ones. Rest in peace.

# CONTENTS

# FOREWORD:
# BISHOP JOHNNY A. TATES

One of the finest experiences in my lifetime, and indeed in my profession as a minister and pastor, was the meeting and acquaintance with Sister Barbara Shephard over fifteen years ago. Reasons for classifying that meeting and subsequent relationship as one of the best and favorite covers several progressive steps. Both of us are long-term employees of Houston area school districts, and thus we share an incisive perspective on educating children. But the dominant thought why I believe our relationship has flourished centers on it being based with undying loyalty and consistent support shown on each other. The truth is that it involves much, much more. I presently serve as Sister Shephard's pastor, and the tears and troubles and tribulations I have shared with her during her personal trials over these fifteen-plus years have proven immeasurable toward our friendship in this joint journey of faith. Succinctly, I was the lecturer of faith. Sister Shephard has been the laboratory specimen, tried and tested over time, and today serves as the conclusive evidence of Scripture as found in Hebrews 11:1 that says "Now faith is the substance of things hoped for and the evidence of things not seen!"

During some of the events described in this book, the reader will discover that the author experienced several diagnoses of contacting cancer and at least two registered at stage 4. I sat in the waiting room with relatives and visited with her throughout, not only surgeries but also through treatments and rehabilitations. I have seen her face pains and watched her exhibit faith that scaled mountains and at the same time walked lonely paths through valleys of the shadows of death that seemed to lead "nowhere." Through her suffering, my own faith grew. Through her tears, my own reasons for crying were altered. While she struggled, my personal walk with the Lord grew.

So herein lies a description of life painted in picturesque words. But it also captures a portrait on canvas laced with faith, tinted with a belief that is actually beyond personal believability, and seasoned with time-proven trust in God that proves too good to be true and yet too fact-filled to be denied.

—Bishop Johnny A. Tates, Senior Pastor
Powerhouse Church of God in
Christ, Houston, Texas

# ACKNOWLEDGMENTS

To the memory of my parents, Jesse and Aslee Shephard. I am thankful that they lived a Christian life before us and encouraged us to do the same. I am thankful for the support and the encouragement that they instilled in me to be the best person I could be.

To my sisters and brothers: JJ, Sealy, Jimmy, George, Bob, Hazel, Mildred, and Glo Baby, thank you for your prayers, untiring love, support, and encouraging words. Thank you for editing my book; you helped me to remember things I had forgotten. You all are the best.

To my nephews/nieces: Gloria, Delores, Michael, Reginya, Roderick, Letecia, James, Jermaine (deceased), Cedric, Felecia, David, DeAndre, Ennis, Natasha, Martin, Mitchell, Nathan, Jonathan, Vincent and Valencia, thank you for being a supporter and an encourager.

To my great nephews/nieces: Darius, Charles, Damien, Jaylin, Vashti, Chandler, Alexa. Josi, Kole, Lauren, J. P., Jazzmine, Anthony, Kaden, Rene, Ava, Vincent, Evans, Breanne, Saniya, Allyssa, and Johnathan, Jr., thank you for being that "special love" in my heart. You always light up my life every time I see you.

To my cousins, thank you for the phone calls, cards, and encouraging words. Every card, phone call/text, or just a "Howdy do?" was so uplifting.

To my pastor and his wife: Bishop and Lady Tates, thank you for your love, support, encouragement, words of wisdom, prayers, and always being available. You will always have a special place in my heart.

To my church family, Powerhouse Church of God in Christ, and other churches thank you for your prayers and showing me so much love.

To my friends: Cheryl Hulett, Sandra Williams, Evelyn Chambers, Lorna Harrison, Angela Shephard, Josi Watkins, Ester Underwood, Shirley Kelly, and Hersey Matthews, thank you for encouraging me to complete my book and taking out the time to edit it. I am also thankful for my best friend, Mosha Marshall (who is now deceased), for editing my book.

To my physicians and all the wonderful people at Hermann Memorial Hospital: the late Dr. Robert Amato, Dr. Tung Shu, Dr. Adrain Rios, Dr. Eva Patton, Dr. Annilisa Gonzales, Dr. Roderick Zvavanjan (Dr. Z), Dr. Helen Lee, and many others. I am thankful for the encouraging words that you all gave me during my illness. You all were so inspiring. You all helped me to believe that things would get better, even when I thought I couldn't make it. Your kindness motivated me to share my story with others.

To my sisters-in-law, nieces-in-law, and nephews-in-laws, thank you all for your prayers, love, kindness, and support.

To two very special people: Xortzy Romano and Machnadbai Rios, thank you all for editing my book. And to Machnadbai, you were so kind to have edited this book even though we have only met through transcripts/notes.

To the doctors, nurses, and complete staff at Deerbrook Dialysis Center, Humble, thank you for being kind, supportive, and helping me to adjust to dialysis. You always make my days go smoothly.

To the Waller District II (Supt. Harold Tisdell and Miss. Ladye Lindsey), thank you all for your prayers, love, kindness, honor, and support. Also, thank you for the special gifts that was presented at the honor service.

# INTRODUCTION

As a child, I was told by my parents that I was a very blessed child. I was told of the many miraculous healings that God performed in my life. This book is compiled of various testimonies and short stories shared by my mother, concerning my miraculous birth and how God spared my life. In this memoir of testimonies, I will share some of the miracles that had a lasting effect in my life. I will also tell you of other miracles that God performed in my family's life. You will find out how I was miraculously healed after twenty-four years of being born with a birth defect. You will also see how God made ways and opened doors in other areas of my life that seemed impossible.

> I will bless the Lord at all times: his
> praise shall continually be in my mouth.
> (Psalm 34:1 KJV)

I once read a book, *Healed of Cancer* by Dodie Osteen. It inspired me so that I also wanted to encourage others. I want to inspire the young as well as the old. I want to help increase their level of faith in God and give others new hope. Sometimes people experience difficult situations and do not realize that others have had similar problems. I want them to know that they are not alone. I am grateful to be able to share my testimonies, and I hope that others, too, will find the same enthusiasm that I felt while writing these testimonies. As you read, you will find humor as well as sorrow. But through all of my situations, you will see the magnificence of God's work.

Many nights, as I sat at my computer and meditated on the greatness of God, I felt the presence of God overshadowing me as I typed. My desire is for God to bless everyone that reads this book. I want them to have a closer walk with him. I want them to realize that if God did it for me, he could do it for them. There is nothing too hard for him. It does not matter who you are; he is capable and able to do whatever we ask of him. We must believe and trust in him.

> For there is no respect of persons with
> God. (Romans 2:11 KJV)

In my lowest moments, you will see how God strengthened me to face some of the greatest obstacles in my life. In 2008, I was diagnosed with *renal cell carcinoma (RCC), stage 4 (kidney cancer)*. In 2012, I was diagnosed with *spinal stenosis with myelopathy* and had to have major surgery. In 2013, *RCC cancer* returned and I had to have three major surgeries. Then in June 2015, I was diagnosed with another cancer, *non-Hodgkin's lymphoma, stage 4*, and had to take chemotherapy for five months. In May 2016, I was told that renal cell carcinoma had returned, and again, I went through surgery. After all of that, I was then diagnosed

THE POWER OF GOD IN A TESTIMONY

with breast cancer, stage 2, in August 2016. I had surgery on October 12, 2016, and then two weeks later because the tumor had metastasized, surgery was done again on December 9, 2016. In 2017, after a year of being cancer free, I was again diagnosed with breast cancer, stage 2. Surgery was successfully performed, and through all of this, God has given me strength to go through. By the grace of God and over ten years later, I am determined to hold on to his hand.

> Behold, I am the Lord, the God of all flesh: is there anything too hard for me? (Jeremiah 32:27 KJV)

I realize that there will come a time that the Lord will call me home, but until then I will not allow my faith to waiver. Through prayers and consecration, I refuse to allow Satan to control or hinder my focus in believing and trusting in God. He has left me here for a purpose, and you will see the miraculous healings of God.

Since I was diagnosed, God has given me a different outlook on life. Every moment is so precious to me. Every day that I wake up, I am reminded that each day is a gift from God and death is just a breath away. Whenever I go to my scheduled doctor's appointments, I go believing and expecting a good report. He keeps proving himself over and over in my life.

> The Lord is not slack concerning his promise. (2 Peter 3:9 KJV)

In spite of the handicap that I was born with and the problems that I have endured, God has blessed me to accomplish many things that some thought were impossible. With God, I know that all things are possible. God works through the impossible. I am a living witness and truly a miracle. As long as I have life, I will continue to trust and testify of his healing power. When I am resting in the arms of God, people can look back and know that God is a healer.

With men this is impossible; but with God all things are possible. (Matthew 19:26 KJV)

Although others have had similar sickness or even worst, God has given me an opportunity to share my story with the world. Sixty-five years later, I am here giving my testimony of what God has done for me. Throughout this book, you will see *the power of God in a testimony.* This is my story.

# CHAPTER 1

# Born to Be a Winner

Jesus said unto him, if thou canst believe,
all things possible to him that believeth.
—St. Mark 9:23 (KJV)

*I Am a Winner*

My life began in a small rural Texas town, west of Houston called Hockley. I was blessed to be born to two wonderful people. I will tell you my story as it was told to me by my mother.

I am the seventh child of nine children: five sisters and three brothers. My parents were married at the age of twenty-one and twenty-two. My dad's name was Jesse Charles Shephard, and my mother had a unique name, which was Aslee Pasalee Alabama Tennessee Shinick-Shephard (she was very fond of her name and it was often a conversation among family and friends). My father was a twin to his brother James. They were born into a large family in which he had many siblings. My mother was the third child of four girls. Both parents worked in the community where my father was a rancher and my mother, a housekeeper.

On the morning of March 7, 1955, my mother went into labor. The hospital was in Houston, which was about an hour away from our home in Hockley. My dad drove swiftly to the Jefferson Davis Hospital to get her there in time. After arriving there, my mother began to have serious complications, besides the normalcy of childbirth. During the process of me being born, she noticed the doctors and nurses anxiously moving around and about the hospital room. She also noticed that after I was delivered, she did not hear the usual cry of a baby that she was accustomed to (after all, I was the seventh child). She then began to pray sincerely and asked God to let everything be all right.

Shortly thereafter, the doctor informed her that I had difficulty breathing. They told her that during delivery, the umbilical cord became detached and I was not breathing on my own. Therefore, I was immediately placed in an oxygen tent. They thought that my chances of surviving were slim. They told her that I had developed a nervous condition because of the lack of oxygen (years later it was diagnosed as a mild case of cerebral palsy). But during this time, my parents kept praying and trusting in God for a healing.

After a very short time, I gradually began to get better. I began to breathe normal and the oxygen tent was removed. That was the first of the many miracles that God would perform in my life. After approximately two weeks, my parents were given permission to take me home. Today, I am writing the testimonies of my life and those close to me.

> And they overcame him by the blood of the Lamb, *and by the word* of their testimony. (Revelations 12:11 KJV)

*Growing-Up Years*

While growing up in the country, we experienced not having an abundance of money, a lot of material things, or lived in the best of houses; but we had a home that was filled with a wealth of love to spread around. God always provided us with our needs. We always had a home to live in, clothes to wear, and food to eat. We never went hungry. My dad owned a few heads of cattle, a few hogs, and few chickens. My mother took care of the chickens on the yard. We were blessed to cultivate our own homegrown garden. We all had different duties. My dad and brothers planted the produce such as: tomatoes, squash, green beans, potatoes, cucumbers, okra, greens, peas, and watermelons. My brothers picked the watermelons while the older siblings picked okra and some of the other vegetables. The younger siblings were responsible for picking the green beans and purple hull peas. I had my share of picking peas. My brothers' other duties were milking the cows, feeding the hogs, chopping wood (for wooden stove), and my sisters' main duties were to sometimes cook, maintain and keep the house clean.

My mother always made sure we were cleaned, with our hair combed and dressed appropriately. Sometimes we wore "hand-me-down" clothes, which we always considered a blessing. We were taught to always be kind and appreciative for whatever others did for us. She often said, "It does not take anything to put a smile on your face or be kind to one another."

> But my God shall supply all your need according to his riches in glory by Christ Jesus. (Philippians 4:19 KJV)

We were always blessed to have enough produce for my family and others. Whenever Dad butchered a cow or hog, he would share over half with family and friends. My dad enjoyed showing and sharing the fruits of his labor. My mother canned a lot of the produce, especially cucumbers and tomatoes. During peach season, she often went to the roadside fruit market, bought peaches by the bushel, and canned them. They were always scrumptiously delicious.

> And also that every man should eat and drink, and enjoy the good of his labour, it is the gift of God. (Ecclesiastes 3:13 KJV)

My parents were very generous, loving, and hardworking people. My dad was willing to give you the shirt off his back, and my mother would give you her last piece of bread. They were always ready to share with others, whether it was support, food, money, or whatever the need was at that time. Many times, I watched my dad help others and give offerings in church that I wondered if he was giving it all. I really believe that some of their generosity spilled over to my siblings and me. Even to this day, we love to have family functions where friends and relatives can come together, socialize, and just enjoy a good time of laughter/fellowship.

"For God loveth a cheerful giver." (2 Corinthians 9:7 KJV)

Living in my household was quite an experience but an enjoyable one. We had a lot of fun, but it had its advantages and disadvantages. I am very blessed to have grown up with great siblings. They are so supportive and unique in their own way. We all had nicknames that many were accustomed to calling us. My dad's boss once said, it seemed like my parents had eighteen children instead of nine. Other people called us by our birth names, but my parents and those close to us called us by our nicknames.

*My siblings and I had different attributes, and here were some:*

*Jessie Lee (JJ)* was the oldest, and we called her our second mom because she always assisted my parents in making sure we had new school clothes ever year.
*Sealy Marie (CC)* became our "Solomon" because she always seemed to solve problems. We asked her opinion, and the problem disappeared.

*James Clarence (Jimmy)* was what we called "easygoing" and softhearted. We could get anything from him by making a sad face and he usually would give us what we wanted.

*George Lawrence (George)* was the repairman. If something simple was wrong with your car or something was broken in the home, he would repair it.

*Robert Ennis (Bob)* was the comedian because he loved to tease. He had a way of making us believe that whatever he said was "true."

*Hazel O'Dee (Dee Cake)* was the one that kept things immaculate. If we left the house in disarray, she told our dad and then we would get a good lecture.

*Barbara Jeanette (Net).* I was the one who always wanted to have the last word in a heated discussion. Since I had a speech impediment, I just wanted to make sure I was understood, so I thought. My dad always quickly reminded me who would have the last word.

*Mildred Jean (Jean)* was the business person. She saved money by leaving hers at home. If we made a short trip to the corner store, she was asked about it. She often responded, "I left my money at home." (Of course, we shared with whatever we had because the next time, she would return the favor). Today, she is a very free-hearted person. As she became older, she assisted my parents in making important business decision.

*Gloria Ann (Glo Baby)* was the youngest one. She had very few responsibilities. She was often teased by us saying she was spoiled and could get away with anything. (She remains spoiled today). She is very smart academically, talent, loves being alone, somewhere reading, writing a book (the author of *Overcoming Grief*), writing biblical skits or plays (her passion).

## Train Up a Child

God saved and baptized my dad with the Holy Ghost while attending the Texas Southwest Church of God in Christ (COGIC) Holy Convocation in Waco, Texas, at the age of eighteen. My mother confessed salvation at the age of twelve and later received the baptism of the Holy Ghost. They loved God, family, church members, and friends. If they had any enemies, I believed they loved them too. They had a deep religious belief, and my dad was also a strong advocate of the church, whether it was time spent in prayer, manicuring the church grounds, or financial support. They believed in devoting their time and resources into making the church a beacon light for others to see Christ.

As years passed, my father later became an ordained deacon at the Good Shepherd COGIC (now known as Victorious Overcomers COGIC) in Hockley, Texas, under the leadership of the late Pastor S. A. Jordan. My mother became the church mother, a position she held until her demise.

My parents had their own distinctive way of rearing and disciplining each one of us. They did not allow us to stay at home from church because we wanted to. We had to have a valid reason. If we were not sick or scheduled to be somewhere else, whenever the car left our home and headed toward church, we were in it.

They taught us at an early age how to pray, trust and believe God, no matter what the situation looks like. God is the answer. I will never forget the many prayers that we had in our home. My dad often assembled us in our family room to pray, where we all gathered on our knees. My family was so large it seemed like we were in a church building. The prayer was often started by us singing the Church of God in Christ (COGIC) anthem, "Yes Lord." Many times, God met us right there in our home. Little did I know, God was preparing me to be able to endure the many difficulties that I would later face in life. Because of their unselfish love to share with others, I believe my siblings and I are recipients of the blessings that God promised. I believe those prayers contributed to me being who I am today.

> The effectual fervent prayer of a righteous man availeth much. (James 5:16 KJV)

They taught us the importance of taking time out for God through fasting, praying, paying tithes, and offering then to wait and see how God blessed financially and, most of all, spiritually.

It was such a joy for me to pay tithes as a child. I did not quite understand the significance of it, but it made me have a very good feeling. I had seen and heard my parents, along with other saints, testifying about the blessings of the Lord, that I just wanted to be a recipient of what God had for me. I was about six or seven years old when I made $1.00 doing an odd job around the house. I was so excited that on the following Sunday, I was able to write my name on a tithing envelope. With my large elementary manuscript, I wrote, "Barbara Shephard, tithes—¢10." Tithing remains a very essential part of my everyday life. Any money that I make or receive, whether it is income or a gift, I give God back 10 percent or more. Since I have stepped out and trusted in his Word, my faith has grown tremendously.

> Bring ye all the tithes into the storehouse, that there may be meat in mine house. (Malachi 3:10 KJV)

My parents dealt with each one of us differently. It was always done with love even though at the time, it did not feel like it. We did not receive a lot of spankings because my father's stern voice would let us know that we had stepped out of bounds. My mother's voice was very soft and easy. I thought she was one of the kindest mothers in the world. I did not want to do anything that would hurt or upset her. I loved her that much. She often corrected us by talking to us by saying, "Do you think God was pleased with that?" or "What are you going to do if Jesus returns while you are doing that?" or "I wouldn't do that if I were you." She put the fear of God in us, but it was always done with affection. She made us think of the consequences of our behavior.

> Train up a child in the way he should go: and when he is old, he will not depart from it. (Proverbs 22:6 KJV)

She always reminded us that Heaven and Hell are real and we needed to choose one or the other. She encouraged us to reverence God in everything we did and often said she did not want us to be lost. So as a child, I tried very hard not to get into much trouble, but many times I found myself misbehaving. If I ever heard her call me by my whole name, "Miss Barbara Jeanette Shephard," I knew that she was displeased with me. So immediately, I tried to correct my behavior. Unfortunately for me, I had to be disciplined more than my other siblings. I seemed to want to keep talking when I was told to be quiet. That was a "no-no" in my home. My parents required "obedience and respect" from each one of us. As I look back over my life, I am thankful that they were consistent in rearing us.

> Withhold not correction from the child. (Proverbs 23:13 KJV)

## A Spiritual Relationship

We attended church very often when growing up although it was just two nights a week. As I got older, I realized attending church that often was a good thing. That was an opportunity for us to see other people that we had not seen since the previous Sunday. There was always plenty of church activities to get involved with, such as Easter and Christmas speeches, church plays, vacation Bible schools, and church picnics.

We spent a lot of time at church. We always got there early, and sometimes we got home at dusk dark. We arrived early because in those days, a wooden heater was used to heat the building. My dad and brothers chopped wood for the heater so the building was warmed and presentable for the arrival of the other saints. Sunday night services were occasionally held because the pastor lived out of town, and it was quite a distance to travel.

Sunday mornings were one of the best days of the week for me because my family was at home and no one had to work. Laughter and chattering could be heard throughout the house. I was often awakened by the radio playing Gospel music and the aroma of my mother cooking Sunday dinner. I can remember vividly her walking through the house with her sweet kind voice saying, "Get up, get up, and get ready to go to Sunday school!" Those words still ring in my ears today. Even as an adult, I realize that Sunday school is a necessity in my life. Usually after a wonderful day in church, the day would end with my relatives coming over to our home and joining in with us to eat dinner and socialize.

We attended many three nights of prayer meetings, and it was during one of those meetings that I surrendered my life to God. It was during the week of Thanksgiving 1980. My pastor, the late Elder Earl Nowlin, was led by God to conduct a "Holiday Revival" at Jordan Memorial COGIC in Hockley, Texas. Elder Samuel Kemper of New York was the revivalist. I was not excited about going because this was my "vacation week," so I thought. My plans were to just go home and relax for the week, but God had greater and other plans for me. During that revival, Elder Kemper preached, so under the anointing, I had a spiritual conviction. After the first night of the revival, I found myself praying and wanting more of God. I desired for him to do something special for me and wanted the fullness of God in my life. I wanted to receive the baptism of the Holy Ghost, and on the last night of the service, God filled me with the Holy Ghost and that with fire and the evidence of speaking with other tongues (Thanksgiving night, November 27, 1980).

> And they were all filled with the Holy Ghost, and began to speak with other tongues, as the spirit gave them utterance. (Acts 2:4 KJV)

I will always be grateful that my parents took us to church instead of sending us. They taught us about God and lived a Christian life before us. They encouraged us to give our life to God at an early age and to know him as our *own* personal Savior. I am thankful to God that today all my siblings confess salvation and they are all active in some area of the church. I give God all the glory because without him and the teaching of my parents, I don't know where we would be.

> Remember now thy Creator in the days of thy youth, while the evil days come not, nor the years draw nigh, when thou shalt say, I have no pleasure in them. (Ecclesiastes 12:1 KJV)

*Fun Summer Days!*

I have many fond memories of the summer months, especially eating those delicious meals with "Kool-Aid" drink or iced tea on a hot day. If my mother cooked fried chicken, steak, liver, spaghetti, or whatever meat, we always had warm homemade biscuits with syrup. Sunday dinners were always special: fried chicken and all the trimmings. Then my mother always topped it off by making some type of dessert, which was usually a homemade cake. After eating a delicious meal, my relatives often came over. We often played softball, kickball, relay races, or what other activity we desired.

On other days, we enjoyed riding bicycles, scooters, running around barefoot on the hot summer sand, making mud pies, and just playing in the warm sun. When it became too hot to play outside, we enjoyed reading books on the front porch, such as *Nancy Drew* series, *The Hardy Boys*, *Bible Stories*, and many more. We had a *Bible Stories* book given to us by our older sister when we were young. We loved, read, and cherished it so much that over the years, the pages became worn and torn.

Christmas Eve and Christmas Day were a very special time in our home. On Christmas Eve, gifts were given to my family from my dad's boss and his wife, the late Mr. and Mrs. Charles Towery (owners of 6T Ranch). After gifts were given, we all gathered around and sang Christmas carols. Later in years, we alternated homes in which Christmas Eve activities were done. This continued until January 1994 (the death of Mr. Charles Towery).

Christmas Day was very exciting. My sisters and I always woke up early with great anticipation, wondering what we got for Christmas. Usually my mother and older sisters had already started preparing the Christmas dinner, turkey and all the trimming. The aroma of turkey, dressing, pies, cakes, etc. filled the house. Before we opened our gifts, my mother would pray and give God thanks for our presents. Then we tore into the wrapping with great joy, always thankful for what we had received.

Television was not a big sport in our home because the only television we had was given to us by someone else. Once the picture tube went out, we would be out of a television for months and sometimes years. Therefore, we did not watch a lot of television. We learned to spend valuable time reading books and novels. Thank God for my late uncle George and aunt Juanita, who lived walking distance from my home. They had a television and we spent two to three hours on weekends watching their television. It felt like their home was our personal theater and so we always looked forward to the weekend so that we could visit them.

For years, my siblings and I have always remained close knit even though we live in our respectful places. When one hurts, we all hurt, and when one is happy, we all are happy. We still get together during various occasions and holidays for family fellowship. It is always a blessing because most of my siblings are now grandparents, and it is a joy spending time with my great nieces and nephews. My siblings are always doing the unexpected, whether it is a birthday, graduation, baby shower, retirement dinner, or just welcome home party. They are just full of surprises. In 2006, I was surprised with a birthday party at the Brady's Landing Restaurant in Houston with over 120 guests in attendance. I have no idea how they kept a secret from me. In 2015, again they surprised me by all of them attending my church at the same time. Unexpectedly, I was the recipient of 2015 Lifetime Achievement Award at the Powerhouse COGIC (Youth Department). I was elated to receive the award and very excited for my family to be present. In September 2019, all my nieces and nephews gave my siblings and I an appreciation banquet called "The 'Nine' Jewels of the Late Jessie and Aslee Shephard." They just wanted to show their kindness and appreciation for what we had done for them over the years. These are the kinds of cherished memories that will be forever seared into my mind.

## Angels Are in Charge

Through all the good times, there were times when we were faced with danger and God protected us through them all. There were two accidents and a near mishap that I vividly remembered while riding the bus to and from school. The first accident happened when my sisters and I were on the bus seated two seats behind the bus driver. As the bus entered the intersection to make a left turn, we heard a horn blowing and a lot of tires screeching. By this time, a truck hit and ripped off part of the front of the bus. If the bus had gone a little farther into the street, it would have hit around the area where we were sitting. I thank God we did not have a single scratch.

The next accident occurred as we were going home from school. Just before the bus stopped to drop off a group of children, we were met by another large truck. This time the road was very narrow with only two lanes and deep ditches on each side. As the bus approached the truck head-on, there was not enough room for either to pass, so the entire bus was forced into the ditch. Thank God the ditches had very little water in it and we were not hurt. We were able to crawl out to safety with assistance.

The third mishap happened when we again were on the bus going home from school. As we approached a railroad crossing, the bus driver did not see the oncoming train. The bus driver began moving forward to cross the tracks, but the kids on the bus began screaming. It startled the bus driver, so he immediately slammed on the brakes. After the bus abruptly stopped, the trained passed in front of the bus within seconds. God spared our lives again. He did then and continues to protect us over and over through seen and unseen situation.

> For he shall give his angels charge over thee, to keep thee in all thy ways. (Psalm 91:11 KJV)

*Divine Indications*

As I got older, I was faced with a serious problem. I had to diligently seek God for guidance. My parents were not around to help me make decisions. I had to depend on God and remember the teachings that I had received.

One day a specific situation came into my life, and it was nagging at me. I had a decision to make, and I had to have the directions from God. I prayed and prayed about it and it seemed like I was not getting an answer.

One evening after arriving home from work, this problem was weighing heavily on my mind. I asked God, "What shall I do?" As I prepared to go to bed, I began to talk and pray sincerely. As I began to pray, I decided to put a "fleece" before God. I asked him to wake me up at four o'clock in the morning because I wanted to spend one hour in prayer. I asked him to wake me up at four o'clock, no matter what it took. I often was a hard sleeper. I wanted God to know I was going to trust him for my answer. My mind was made up. I needed to hear from God concerning this problem. After I prayed, I dozed off to sleep.

During that night, my telephone rang. Drowsy, I reached over and answered the phone. It was a man's voice that I did not recognize and he said, "Hello!" I responded by saying, "Hello…hello…hello!" He did not respond, so by this time I woke up completely because it frightened me. He did not say anything else; I decided that I should hang up. I thought that someone might be playing on the phone or he had the wrong number. As I was about to hang up, he said, "Well, Barbara, I am going to let you go." He hung up the phone before I could say anything.

By this time, I was really awakened. I could not imagine who was calling me and knew my name. In the darkness of my room, I glanced over at the clock to see the time. The clock said four o'clock. Immediately, I remembered what I had asked God for before going to sleep. I rolled out of my bed, unto my knees, and began to pray. When I got off my knees, I looked backed at the clock and it said five o'clock. God answered me that night. That problem that I was confronted with, God solved that too.

# CHAPTER 2

# God's Miraculous Healings

And with his strips we are healed.
—Isaiah 53:5 (KJV)

*Dad's Healing*

As a child, I always had this belief that God could do the impossible, only if I believe. One of the first miracles that I was able to see and witness with my own eyes was my dad's healing. I was twelve years old when he was diagnosed as having a severe massive stroke.

We lived in the country (rural area) in a frame house with a large front porch. It was a place we loved to sit in the cool of the day while reading, talking, and playing. It was on June 7, 1967 when I was awakened to a lot of unusual noise. I tried to focus my thoughts from being asleep when I noticed the noise was coming from my parents' bedroom. Confused and not knowing what was going on, I got up out of bed and went outside to the front porch. My parents' bedroom window was adjacent to the front porch. We had no air conditioner, so the window was raised. There I had a better view and I could see what was going on. The noise that I heard was my mother and older siblings praying around my fathers' bedside.

As I peered through the opened screened window, I could see that he was just lying on the bed with a very strange stare on his face. He was not saying a word or responding in any way. That was when I knew something was wrong. It seemed like he was gasping for air. My mother tried to shield me and my younger sisters from seeing what was going on. I became very curious and started to cry. I began questioning my older sisters as what was happening. Then they told us that Dad was very ill and my brother George had already gone to call for the ambulance. My parents did not have a telephone, so it took a while for the ambulance to arrive. My brother had to drive about half mile to use a neighbors' telephone. The ambulance did arrive about thirty minutes later and took him to the Waller County Hospital in Hempstead, Texas. He was examined and diagnosed as having a severe massive stroke at the age of forty-eight.

Many of my fathers' friends were notified, and they came in and out to pray for him. Others elsewhere were also praying. The younger siblings and I were not allowed to go to the hospital, so we stayed at home while waiting to hear more news. That was one of the longest and saddest days in my life. Finally, that afternoon my siblings came home and gave us more details of what was taking place. We were told that Dad was paralyzed and seriously ill. They were stabilizing him and was going to transport him to the medical center in Houston. Later that evening, he was transferred to the Methodist Hospital in Houston, Texas.

After arriving there, the doctors immediately began to examine him to determine the extent of his illness. He remained in critical condition for about three to four weeks and not responding to anyone. The doctor told my mother and family that he was very critical. A blood clot was detected near his brain and it was too close to the brain to perform surgery. They were going to watch his progress very closely, and hopefully the blood clot would dissolve, but would do whatever could be done to keep him comfortable. Our family, friends, and church members continued to fast, pray, and seek God.

Finally, after about a month and a half, my younger sisters and I were able to visit our dad. It was very difficult for us to see him so sick. It was then that I understood why my mother did not want us to see him. He had lost so much weight and did not look the same. Gradually, his health became better and he remained in Methodist Hospital for about three months. Upon leaving the hospital, he was sent to a rehabilitation center. There by the help of God, each day he got better and stronger.

After many weeks of therapy, on November 3, 1967, Dad was discharged to go home. God performed a miracle in his life. He did not ever have surgery, and the blood clot dissolved and disappeared. He returned home with no mental side effects. He only had a few physical limitations, but after continuation of therapy, his health improved even more. After many months of therapy, he once again was able to do many things that he had previously done: walk, talk, run, and drive without any assistance. If a stranger would have ever seen him on the streets, they would have never known that he was once a severe stroke patient. There were no physical signs of him ever having a stroke. God is a miracle worker. Dad was blessed to live an active and productive life sixteen more years.

> With long life will I satisfy him, and shew him my salvation. (Psalm 91:16 KJV)

In February 1983, Dad suffered a massive heart attack. After about three weeks of being ill, the Lord called him home on February 22, 1983. We were blessed to have had him in our lives. He was sixty-four years old.

*Wow! I Am Healed!*

When I was much younger, I was easily embarrassed because the right side of my face, right arm, and right hand had uncontrollable movements (tremors). It bothered me both physically and mentally. It was hard to do simple things: hold a glass of milk without spilling it or just trying to write my name on a piece of paper. I did not like when others saw me that way, and I sometimes became irritated when asked about it, which led to me being withdrawn from my peers. Using it as a defense mechanism, I learned how to change the conversation or just ignore them.

As I got older, I noticed that the uncontrollable movements became worse. I visited different doctors on several occasions to see if I could be helped. I was examined, various tests were done, and my previous medical records were reviewed. The doctors determined that because of the lack of oxygen during birth, I had a mild case of cerebral palsy. But deep within, I knew in my heart that God was going to heal me. Since my mother told me about my birth, I knew God had his hand on my life and I believed that he had a purpose for me. As years passed, I just kept praying, believing that one day my miracle would take place. Finally, that day came.

> Heal me, O Lord, and I shall be healed. (Jeremiah 17:14 KJV)

During a Texas Southwest Church of God in Christ (COGIC) Revival in Houston, God wrought a miracle in my life, after twenty-four years of an affliction. I wrote an article in *The King's Messenger* (a Christian newspaper) on September 1979 titled "I'm Healed," and it reads:

### I'm Healed

On August 9, 1979, at Texas Southwest Revival in Houston, the Lord healed me of a nervous condition. I had this affliction since birth. The right side of my body trembled (right side of face, arm and hand) most of the time. The doctors or medicine would not do me any good. I trembled so bad, that when I was a child, it was an embarrassment for me to eat in public or hold a glass of water for fear I would spill it. I began to seek more professional help. The doctors ran tests, but never could come up with a way to solve it. After entering college in 1973, I began to accept whatever it was and make the best out of it. But instead, the trembling got worse. It moved into my right leg and foot making things more complicated. Again, I accepted it and was determined to make the best out of life. Oh, but on that Thursday night, after a year and 3 months out of college, I accepted something else. Thank God, I accepted my healing.

After Bishop F. D. Washington of Brooklyn, New York finished preaching, he turned the service over to Bishop T. D. Iglehart. Bishop Iglehart called for a prayer line for the sick. I didn't get in line that night, because I wasn't suffering with anything unusual. So I sat in the choir stand and looked on others as they went through the line. But, there was one particular person my eyes were fastened upon. It was Supt. Thomas Johnson. I noticed him laying hands on the sick and then he got in line. As I looked at him going through the line I noticed a difference. By the time he got to the front of the prayer line, the power of the Lord touched him and he shook as if someone had put an electric shock on him. After he took his seat, I noticed his eye lids weren't trembling. I began thanking the Lord for touching his eyes, not knowing that was his healing he would later testify of. As he began to testify of what the Lord had done for him, I felt the power of God touch my body and I began praising the Lord for my healing. I looked at my hand and noticed it was not trembling. I went home that night claiming my healing. I didn't tell anyone about my hand, I wanted to be sure. During the night, I would awake saying, "Thank the Lord, I'm healed." The next morning I got up saying, "I'm healed." As I went about my daily task, I noticed that my hand still was not trembling. Again I said, "I'm healed. Thank the Lord." I couldn't keep it to myself any longer. The first person that I talked to that day, I told about God had done for me. Today, I am yet healed and can do things with my hand that I have never been able to do. I know for myself that God still works miracles.

*Whose Report Do You Believe?*

Nearly twenty-nine years later, I received some dev-astating news. I was diagnosed with renal cell carcinoma, stage 4 (kidney cancer). I was so distraught that I felt my life was over, and I felt my future was doomed.

It all started with me having severe back pains, which I had suffered for many years, and the pains continued to grow worse. I visited doctors after doctors, but the pain persisted. Finally, I found a rheumatologist that took an interest in my case. After reviewing my medical records, she immediately ordered me to have an MRI on my entire back and abdomen.

On April 14, 2008, an MRI was performed. After a few days, the results showed that I had a slipped disc and I would need to have injections to help ease the pains; also the test detected that there were two nodules on my left kidney. The rheumatologist told me that it didn't look very serious, but I should contact a urologist as soon as possible. School was nearing the end for the summer vacation, so I decided to wait to take care of it. On June 9, 2008, I made the appointment and saw the urologist. As he looked at the results of my reports, his face looked concerned. He ordered to see all previous CT scans to compare. After reviewing all scans, an ultrasound of my left kidney was ordered immediately. Later, the results were in and the test showed that there was a tumor detected on my left kidney and it looked cancerous; but it could not be determined until a biopsy was done. The biopsy was scheduled and done on July 3, 2008.

Later during the next week, I received a called from the office of the urologist. They asked me to come into the office on that same evening. With fear trying to grasp my mind, my sisters and nephew Martin accompanied me to the doctor's office. I did not want to be alone when the results were given. The urologist came in and discussed the diagnosis with us. He told us that the tumor was malignant and recommended another urologist that was an expert with cases like mine. He urged us to see the specialist as soon as possible. I had cancer and what do I do?

> Who healeth all thy disease. (Psalm 103:3 KJV)

I was speechless. I began to cry with sorrow because it seemed like my world had turned upside down. My family and I walked out of the doctor's office with very few words. My mind was in deep thought, and I just wanted to be alone. I knew of no one in my immediate family with cancer and I began to wonder, "Lord, why me?" It felt like my life was ending and I could not even imagine me having a future. I tried to pray, but it seemed as though God was not to be found.

When we returned home, it felt like I had lost a loved one, but I thank God for my family. They assured me that we were going to get through this with the help of God. They encouraged me to pick myself up and not to lose faith. After listening and talking with them awhile, I stopped, thought, and came to myself. With tears in my eyes, I began to give God thanks, even when I did not understand. I knew God was in control of everything, and I just had to trust him.

> In everything give thanks: for this is
> the will of God in Christ Jesus concerning
> you. (1 Thessalonians 5:18 KJV)

## *I Believe God's Report*

Incidentally, on the same day I received the news, I was scheduled to attend Vacation Bible School (VBS) that evening at my church (Powerhouse COGIC, Houston, Texas). I really did not want to go that night, but my sister urged me. They thought that it would help lift my spirits by being with others. Thank God I believed that was the best medicine for me at that time. It truly was a blessing being with the other church members.

After VBS, I told some of the church members about the report, and they immediately began to pray with me. I am thankful for such wonderful members at my church, particularly the pastor and his wife, Pastor/Bishop Johnny A. Tates and Lady Lee Tates. They are truly and still are a blessing to me.

> Is any sick among you? Let him call
> for the elders of the church; and let them
> pray over him, anointing him with oil in
> the name of the Lord. (James 5:14 KJV)

When VBS was over, I went into the church office to have a conference with my pastor and his wife. I was somewhat still in the state of shock, but as they began to pray and minister to me, my fear began to vanish. They gave me words of encouragement and kept reassuring me that everything was going to be all right. They blessed me with such powerful words of wisdom that night that when I left church, my spirit was uplifted and has remained uplifted. God gave me strength, peace of mind, and removed that fear that was trying to torment me.

> Fear thou not; for I am with thee:
> be not dismayed; for I am God: I will
> strengthen thee; yea, I will help thee.
> (Isaiah 41:10 KJV)

The appointment was made and along with my family met with the new urologist, Dr. Tung Shu (one of the finest urologists in Houston). After my records were reviewed, the alternatives were discussed with my family and me. It was recommended to me to have laparoscopic surgery. He then told us how it would be done. He explained that a nephrectomy (kidney is partially or completely removed) would be taking place. We were told that the tumor looked very small and it seemed to be contained in one area. They thought it would take several years before it grew large enough to metastasis. Since the tumor was so small, it was not necessary to have surgery right away, but I was encouraged to have surgery within a year. I left the doctor's office, went home, and did more research on the doctor and the diagnosis before making final preparation for surgery.

The day finally arrived, and on September 23, 2008, my family and I arrived at Memorial Hermann Hospital in Houston, Texas, to be admitted. My surgeon, Dr. Shu, came in and finalized with us what would be taking place during surgery. He again told us that the surgery was being done laparoscopic. He believed that procedure was less invasive and fewer side effects usually occurs. He informed us approximately how long the surgery and recovery would be.

As the time approached for me to go into surgery, fear again tried to grasp my mind. But thank God for my sister Mildred who was with me in the prep room at that time. She whispered a word of prayer with me, and God once again gave me a peace of mind. When we got to the operating room, they put me on the table, and just before they gave me anesthetic, my mind was at ease. I believed in my heart that I was in God's hand and everything was going to be all right.

> And he said unto me, My grace is suf-
> ficient for thee: for my strength is made
> perfect in weakness. (2 Corinthians 12:9
> KJV)

During surgery, the surgeons discovered that the cancer had metastasized to one of my lymph nodes. Immediately, partial of left kidney and the lymph node were removed. After surgery, my family was told we needed to see an oncologist on the following week to determine what treatments would be used. With that news I was devastated, but I knew I had to trust in God. He recommended one of the best oncologists in Houston, the late Dr. Robert Amato. I remained in the hospital approximately five days. While being there, I thank God for the visits from family, pastor, his wife, and friends. They all helped uplift my spirit during those gloomy moments.

I was taken home and began the slow process of getting well. The next week, I was taken to see the late Dr. Amato, and he informed us that it was renal cell carcinoma (RCC), stage 4 (kidney cancer). He discussed what would take place over the next five years. We asked him about chemotherapy, but he told us that RCC was resistant to chemotherapy. He explained that there was a medication that could control it for a certain amount of time. He ordered that I have another CT scan in two weeks, and after that, he would determine what treatments would be necessary to use.

## God Is a Healer

During this time, I was surrounded by family and friends that continued to give me the support I needed. I was especially thankful for my pastor and his wife, Bishop Johnny and Lady Tates. They were very inspirational to me and my family throughout this ordeal and remain that way today. Even in my lowest moments, they were there to pray and exhilarate me. When I went home and was recuperating, they continued to call, send notes, and got updates on my recovery. I am reminded of words that Bishop Tates once said to me, "You do not have to get sick for God to let you die." Those words were important to me and have become a part of my everyday life. I believe that God placed them in my life for such a time as this, and I am eternally grateful.

Two weeks passed, CT scans had been done and once again I visited my oncologist. The results were reviewed with me and my family. As he began to show and explain the films of the CT scans to us, my spirit was uplifted. He said they could not see any more cancer. They could only see where the cancer had been (could see the staples and swelling of the area). I stood there confused and not understanding exactly what he meant. We then asked about the treatments that were used for cancer patients. Again, he replied that there was no need for any treatments because there was no cancer to target. As I stood in his office with my family, I responded out loudly, "Thank you, Jesus!" That was all I could say. As we sat in his office, he continued to explain the results and told me to come back in six weeks.

In the meantime, Dr. Shu, my urologist, informed us that my siblings should have an ultrasound to determine if cancer was present in their bodies. He told us that if one sibling had it, there was a good chance another might have it. I knew God had performed another miracle in my life. I left out of the doctor's office with a smile on my face and praise in my heart. I began making telephone calls with tears of joy in my eyes, telling others of what God had done for me. Even to this day, I am yet testifying of my healing.

He sent his word, and healed them.
(Psalm 107:20 KJV)

I followed the doctors' orders, scheduled another CT scan, and returned in six weeks. Again, the results showed "no cancer." I was then told that I should always follow up and report for the next five years for more CT scans. I was encouraged to report as following: first and second year, report every three months; third year, report every four months; fourth year, report every six months; and fifth year, report once a year.

During one of my checkups in May 2009, another mass was detected on my right kidney. Again, along with my pastor, family and friends, we went to God in prayer. I was truly thankful for my dear friend and coworker Evelyn Chambers. She had previously gone through a similar ordeal, and her words of encouragement came at the right time. She had been "cancer free" for four years.

Another biopsy was taken, and thank God, the results showed that it was benign. Through prayer, God continues the work he had started in my life, and I will tell others and testify of his greatness. It has been over ten years since I was first diagnosed with cancer, but with the help of God, I am still here. I give God all the glory.

*God Keeps Healing*

In May 2012, my faith was again tested. I woke up early on a Sunday morning with excruciating pain in my left neck, shoulder, and arm. It was very painful to move about, and I could not get any relief. I was not able to do anything without assistance. Later that evening, I went to emergency, and the doctor took test and gave me some morphine to help ease the pain. That only lasted a little while and the pain soon returned.

After about a week, the pain became worse. I was taken to emergency again, but this time I was hospitalized. A specialist was called in, and after many X-rays, scans, and MRI, it was determined that I had a medical disorder called spinal stenosis with myelopathy (spinal disorder). I was told by the doctor that it was good I came in when I did because it could have led to me being paralyzed. Three days later, I had major surgery. After surgery, my blood pressure became uncontrollably high, so I was taken to the critical care unit (CCU). My sister Hazel remained by my bedside throughout the night. After two days, my blood pressure began to level off to normalcy and I was sent to a regular room. Gradually, I became better. I had to learn over how to comb my hair, pick up objects from the floor, button my clothes, and walk without assistance. After twelve days, I was discharged from the hospital, and it took about a year before I regained full use of my left arm and hand. God had done it again.

In February 2013, after my regular checkup, I was told by my oncologist that the renal cell carcinoma (cancer) had returned. The news was hard to hear but not as devastating as it was the first time. Over the years, my faith had gotten stronger. I knew God was a healer because he had done it so many times before. This time, the cancer was in both kidneys, one on the right and two on the left. I would need to have surgery, but the procedures would be done in three different intervals. The new procedure was called *cryoablation.* This is when the tumors (cancer cells) are frozen by doing laparoscopic surgery. The surgeries were scheduled and performed in June, July, and September. After a summer of being ill, God brought me out all right. On December 2, 2013, I returned for my CT scans, MRI, and follow up with my oncologist. My results were read and given to me and once again, I was given a good report: "cancer free."

During the summer of 2014, I began to have shortness of breath while walking short distances and I always felt sluggish. I began to lose unexplainable weight and my sleep habits changed. I went to my oncologist and he referred me to my nephrologist (kidney specialist). Over the summer, I kept going back and forth for doctor's appointments without any relief. Finally, on August 20, 2014, I was hospitalized. I was told by my doctor that I now had *end-stage renal disease* because of my kidney functions that I had over the last few years. He told me it was time to start dialysis. It was a little disappointing, but I had been told that this day would probably come. With regret, I began dialysis treatments, and I now take dialysis three hours, three days a week. It has been challenging, and some days are worse (very weak) than other, but God keeps giving me the strength to go on. Even though I have a blood transfusion every six to eight weeks, I am trusting God for complete healing. One thing that keeps me going is I realize how blessed I am. There are many others that are sicker than me. Every challenge I endure, I know God is with me; so every day I give him the praises.

*Miraculous Healings of My Siblings*

As suggested by Dr. Shu, my siblings went to the doctor and had ultrasounds on their kidneys. Sure enough, one of my sisters tested positive. January 2009, my second oldest sister, Sealy, was told that a tumor was detected on her right kidney and it, too, might be malignant. She was devastated, but she had faith that God would do for her what he had done for me.

She also had concerns because she was so close to reaching a milestone in her life. She had always wanted to earn a master's degree, and at the age of sixty-five years old, she was in the process of doing just that. She did not want to drop out, so we began to pray and believe God. We knew that this was just another test. God had done it before in my life, and we believed he would do it again in her life. She had a biopsy done, and surgery was scheduled for April 2009. She was diagnosed with renal cell carcinoma (RCC), stage 1. She had surgery, and the cancer was successfully removed from her kidney. They asked her to report back for checkups once a year.

God granted her desire, and just two months after surgery, June 2009, she was blessed to graduate with a master's degree from Colorado Tech University, Colorado Springs, Colorado. Upon completion of her getting a master's degree, she had a longing in her heart to work on her doctorate degree. In January 2011, she entered the doctorate program at Colorado Tech University.

In November 2014, approaching graduation again, she received devastating news: RCC (cancer) had returned.

Surgery was scheduled as soon as possible. Surgery was done, but this time her right kidney was successfully removed. While recuperating a few days, she was able to continue with her studies. Once again, after follow-ups with her doctors, she was "cancer free." Her faith had not waivered, and she continues to tell others about her healing. She knew that God was in control of her life. Through all of that, she was blessed to complete her dissertation and graduate with a degree in Doctorate in Management (DM) in December 2014 at the age of seventy-one. To God be the glory!

On March 31, 2015, just as I was getting used to dialysis, I had to be hospitalized again. I was not able to be dialyzed because the graft in my arm became clogged. I had to have surgery to place a catheter in my chest to resume dialysis. In the meantime, my brother Jimmy was also in the hospital/rehabilitation with kidney complications. We were all in prayer for him.

The next day, as I waited to have my procedure done, I received startling news. My brother Robert (Bob) became seriously ill. He was at work, talking to his coworkers, when he collapsed suddenly. His coworkers thought it was an April Fools' joke since it was April 1. Then they noticed that this was not a joke. Immediately they started performing CPR and called 911. The EMTs worked on him several minutes and then transferred him to Memorial Hermann Hospital in the Woodlands, Texas. After arriving there, he was taken to the intensive care unit (ICU) where the doctors put him in a medically induced coma. He was diagnosed as having a cardiac arrest. He had no blockage. The doctors said his heart just stopped beating. He remained in a coma for about six days. During this time, our family and friends kept praying and believing God for the best.

On that same day, my sister Mildred had not been feeling well; she decided to drive herself to emergency. After arriving there, she was examined and immediately admitted to St. Luke's Hospital, Houston. There was a large amount of fluid around her heart and the doctors told her emergency surgery was needed as soon as possible. Major surgery was done on her heart, and she remained in the hospital for nine days. After a few weeks of recuperation, God healed her, and later she returned to home and back to work.

During this time, Bob remained in ICU for about nine days. As he gradually became better, he was transferred out of ICU to a regular room. He began to identify people, talked, walked, and regained his strength. After a few more days in the hospital, he was transferred to TTRR Rehabilitation at Memorial Hermann Hospital. After many days of therapy, he was discharged to go home on April 27, 2015. He left the hospital walking, talking, and in his right mind. If you saw him today, you would have never known what he had gone through and he was right at death's door. God did it again. He is truly a miracle worker. I am so thankful for my siblings; they faithfully made rounds to visit each one of us. We were so blessed to be able to depend on them for support.

Then in May 2015, the unexpected happened. My sister Hazel went to her regular checkup and was told that she had breast cancer, stage 2, and surgery was needed as soon as possible. I did not quite understand what and why all of this was happening to my immediate family. But in my heart, I knew God was in control. So along with my family, friends, and church members, we kept praying and believing God. As the surgery was being done, the doctors detected that cancer was in both breasts. Instead of her having a single mastectomy, the doctors performed a double mastectomy. She was on chemotherapy for four months and radiation for six weeks. God healed her; "cancer free" and after several months at home, she was able to return to work. She worked until retirement, August 2018. God worked another miracle.

During that same year my health started to decline again. It was hard to eat or hold food on my stomach, and I continued to lose weight. I did not know why I had no appetite. I was hospitalized several times in April and May for different tests and scans because the doctors were trying to determine exactly what was wrong with me. Finally, June 2015, I was diagnosed with non-Hodgkin's lymphoma, stage 4 (cancer). It had already metastasized to my bowels (intestine area), spine, and left lung. It felt like I had been hit with a sledgehammer. I did not know what to do but go to God in prayer. I knew he had healed me several times before even though I continued to rapidly lose weight. I just believed God for whatever I was going to face. I began chemotherapy treatments which lasted five months. I continued to lose weight, losing over one hundred pounds, and lost all my hair; but I kept my faith in God. As of October 2015, I was blessed to finally ring the bell and once again I was "cancer free." Thank God, another miracle was performed.

A year later, May 2016, I had my usual three-month checkup concerning my kidneys. The regular tests and scans were done. After the results came back, it was determined that RCC (kidney cancer) had returned. Surgery was scheduled and performed on June 24, 2016. This time, since I had lost so much weight, there were complications during surgery. Afterward, I was told by the surgeon that they had great concerns about completing the surgery. Surgery lasted nearly seven hours compared to the usual five hours in the past. I came out "cancer free."

During that same year, my brother George had a nagging cough that had been nagging at him for a while. After a few months, he decided to go to the doctors and get it checked out. He followed up with different doctors' appointments, test, MRIs, and scans. Finally, the results came in, and he was told that he had colon cancer, stage 2. Again, that took my family by surprise, but our faith became stronger in God. He had proven himself too many times in our lives. It was no use in doubting him now. In June 2016, surgery was scheduled and done with a few complications. He remained in the Methodist Hospital/ Rehabilitation, Houston for about three weeks. He was given chemotherapy treatments for four months. All reports have shown that he also is now "cancer free." Another miracle was performed.

Nearing the end of summer, August 2016, I had my yearly mammogram. After results were in, I was told to come back for another mammogram and biopsy. Fear tried to grasp my mind again, but I knew I had to trust God. I felt that I had been through so much, and I wondered if

I could anymore. I knew God was the only answer, and I must continue to believe in his healing power. Later the results came in and the diagnosis was breast cancer, stage 2. On October 12, 2016, surgery was performed. God brought me through surgery and later I went home to recuperate. Two weeks later, I returned for a follow-up, but the news was upsetting. The tumor in my breast had metastasized and surgery would need to be done again. With that news, my heart just seemed to sink. My words were few, and my mind was in deep thought. I knew God would not put more on me that I could bear, but it seemed like my faith was weakening. Thank God for my family, close friends, my pastor and his wife, Bishop and Lady Tates. They began to pray and gave me more encouraging words. Some way and somehow, my strength became renewed. Surgery was performed again on December 9, 2016. The tumor was removed successfully, and since the tumor had metastasized, I was required to take radiation for six weeks. After radiation was completed, I was once again "cancer free." Again, another miracle was worked.

Nearly a year had passed when I went back for my yearly checkup. Tests, scans, ultrasounds, and MRI were taken. When the results were reported, I was told that my breast cancer had returned. Again, I went through surgery on December 5, 2017, and the tumor was successfully removed. God worked another miracle in me.

Thou will keep him in perfect peace,
whose mind is stayed on thee: because he
trusteth in thee. (Isaiah 26:3 KJV)

Then in February 2018, I again began feeling very weak and just sick. I could not shake the feeling. The doctor decided to hospitalize me to see what was wrong. After different tests and scans, I was told that I had a blood infection. The doctors were concerned because they could not tell where it was coming from. I had a high fever, and they continued to give me more test. Finally, the fever came down to normalcy. I was hospitalized for seven days, and they never found out what caused the blood infection. God brought me through that.

In February 2018, after forty-eight years of living in Los Angeles, California, my sister Sealy decided to move back home to Texas. Her husband, Edward, had passed away, and she really did not have much family left there. She felt that it was time once again to be closer to family. Just before she moved, she became sick and had to have test done. After arriving home, she found new doctors in Houston and decided to have more tests done. After many test, MRI, and scans were completed, she was diagnosed with Hodgkin's lymphoma, stage 2. Again, we all went to God in prayer. We knew God was a healer because he had proven himself to us too many times before. God blessed her to go through the treatments (chemotherapy and radiation) successfully. As of February 2019, she too testified that she was "cancer free." Even though she continued to battle other ailments (congestive heart failure and diabetes), her faith became much stronger.

On July 31, 2020, sadly after battling congestive heart failure (results of chemotherapy and radiation) and other ailments, Sealy passed in South Houston Hospice,

Houston, Texas. Our hearts were heartbroken, but we knew that God's will must be done. We knew she was in better hands and that she was no longer suffering in pain and having sleepless night. My parents were blessed with nine children, and she was the first sibling to pass, so we had much to be thankful for. She had just turned seventy-seven years old on July 7, 2020. She and her smile will truly be missed. Rest in peace, our sister!

In August 2018, I went for my checkup because it was time for my colonoscopy. I was examined, but this time, polyps were detected on my colon and I had to have surgery. It was too dangerous to remove without major surgery. They were concerned whether it was cancerous or not. They would not know until after surgery. On September 5, 2018, surgery was performed. They removed about eight inches of my colon, and thank God, it was "not cancer." I remained in the hospital and went home a few days later.

After my sister's death in July 2020, I noticed that my health began to give me problems. I could not sleep well, had shortness of breath, consistent cough, very weak, and had to use a walker to walk. (I had a COVID test five times, and all results came back negative). I went to ER several times, but each time, the doctors seemed not to be able to find the problem. Usually, I was given different medications to take to no avail.

In November 2020, it was time for my yearly checkup concerning cancer. I had test done and another tumor was detected on my kidney (RCC). Other tests were done, and it was determined that surgery was needed. Surgery was scheduled for January 14, 2021, but before surgery, I had to have other tests done for clearance. In December 2020, the cardiologist examined me. I was then told that I had congestive heart failure (CHF) because of past chemo and radiation. That is why I had shortness of breath, coughing, and weaknesses. Kidney (RCC) surgery had to be postponed until later. I was given a stress test and checked for blockage. Thank God there was no blockage, and on January 14, 2021, I was given a cardiac clearance for surgery. Kidney (RCC) is scheduled for me later.

When I was first told that I had CHF, the human side of me became very depressed. But deep within my spirit, I knew God was a healer and was in control of this situation. No matter what happens, I know God is still with me. As I began to talk and ask questions, I told the doctor to be honest with me. I wanted to know the scale of my sickness and what was the life expectancy for me. I was told, and some medical knowledge was shared with me. Then tears began to well up in my eyes. But suddenly, the doctor got my attention by saying, "You are living by the grace of God, and God has a purpose in your life." Then the doctor began quoting uplifting scriptures one after another to me. It was so uplifting to me that I stopped feeling depressed and began to thank God for what he had already done for me. My mind has been made up as I go through this again. I will continue to trust and believe God. He has done too much for me. My hope is in God. My prayer is to live so I can see God's face in peace. I am living this life to live again.

After all I had been through in 2020, I was hit with another hard blow. On Sunday, February 7, 2021, I woke up early with excruciating pains in my stomach. I could not get any rest, so I went to the emergency at the hospital. After being examined by the doctors, I was told that I had a hernia that needed to be repaired immediately. But there was a problem, I was a high risk patient due to congestive heart failure. I was told that if we went into surgery, I probably would not survive. My faith began to weaken. I knew God was able and I needed him to intercede for me then. I was alone, frightened and did not know what to do, after I was told that I might not survive through the night if I had surgery. I began to call my pastor, family, and friends. I shared with them the situation I was facing. Thank God, they began to pray and seek God on my behalf.

While staying in the hospital six days, different specialist came in to examine my case. It was finally determined that emergency surgery was not needed at the time, but surgery would need to be done as soon as possible. Meantime, I had the opportunity to go home, pray, talk with my family and think on what decisions that I would have to make. I knew that I was high risk and whatever decision I would make was going to be dangerous.

After returning home from the hospital, I began to pray and seek God like I have never done before. I began to search my life for anything that was not pleasing to God. I asked God to remove all things that was not like him. I knew in my heart that God was in control of my life and if God called me, I wanted to see his face in peace.

One day as I was sitting and meditating, a peace came over me. The scripture came to my mind. 2 Corinthians 5:8 (KJV)says, "We are confident, I say, and willing rather to

be absent from the body, and to be present with the Lord."
I began to thank God on how he healed and spared my life
so many times. I told my family that after much prayer, my
decision was that I would have the surgery. I told them I
had put it in God's hand. If I woke up after surgery, it was
good and if I did not it was good. In my heart, I realized
what 2 Corinthians 5:8 (KJV) meant. On March 16, 2021,
I had the surgery that repaired the hernia and surgery came
out successfully. That is why I continue to give God the
praise. Even though I am being faced with other challenges
(congestive heart failure and kidney surgery) in 2021, I am
trusting in God. One thing I know is that God is capable
to bring me out.

As I look back over my life, I truly believe that God
has a purpose for me. I was very distraught when I was
first told that I had cancer; but I did not realize how it was
going to help others and especially those so dear to me. If
I had not gone through my affliction, my siblings would
have never gone to have ultrasounds done on their kidneys.
I have learned that God sometimes permit us to go through
some things to help others.

And we know that all things work
together for good to them that love God.
(Romans 8:28 KJV)

# CHAPTER 3

# There's Power in Knowledge

The fear of the Lord is the
beginning of knowledge.
—Proverbs 1:7 (KJV)

*Education Is Needed*

My parents' education was limited because they had to withdraw from school at a very young age. They both dropped out while they were in elementary. Their employment was working in the fields, which was usually picking cotton. After my dad and mother married, he became a farmer on a ranch, and my mother became a housekeeper in different homes in the community.

They always wanted better for my siblings and me, so they were very much involved in our education. They made sure that they became acquainted with the school administration and had great concerns about the schools' curriculum. They wanted to know what kind of activities that we would be involved in. Again, my parents had very little education, but they were well-respected in the community and by the school administrators. My dad was once asked to give the invocation at my oldest sister's graduation, which was an honor. (In those days, if you were not educated, that opportunity was rare).

Even though some of us were not professing salvation, they wanted the school personnel to know what they expected out of us as children coming from a Christian home. They wanted us to be trustworthy, even when we were not in their presence. My mother always reminded us by saying, "Whatever you choose to do or how successful you become in life, don't forget God. Always put God first and remember from whence you came. Trust and see God for all of your directions."

> In all thy ways acknowledge him, and
> he shall direct thy paths. (Proverbs 3:6 KJV)

As my siblings and I grew older, we understood what our parents were trying to instill in our lives. We wanted to make them proud. I remembered vividly at one of my sibling's college graduation. The president of the university asked for the parents to stand if they had two or more children that had graduated from that university. My mother stood with a smile on her face and with joy in her heart; that left me with a good impression. I always wanted to make her happy. Five of my siblings had completed college at that time. They wanted us to be young people that grew up to be respectful and productive in society, but, above all, to know God for ourselves. They encouraged each one of us to strive to make good grades in school and continue to further our education by attending schools of higher learning. Most of us were blessed to go to Prairie View A&M University, Prairie View, Texas, to further our education. It was in proximity of our home. We were able to live at home and maintain a job. I did not have a car, but my dad always made a way for me to get there or he would take me back and forth. It was their endeavor for each one of us to get better jobs and be successful in life. I am so thankful that before Dad and Mother went home to be with the Lord, I had an opportunity to let them know how much I appreciated their steadfastness.

> Give me now wisdom and knowledge. (2 Chronicles 1:10 KJV)

## Salvation Is a Necessity

Many times, I thought they were too strict, but as I reminisce back, it did not harm us. They were doing all that they knew. It made us better children and adults. They never had to get us out of jail or go to the school because of discipline problems. The other students knew what our parents stood for, and they respected our beliefs, and the teachers did abide by our parents' wishes. We were never forced to be a part of something that we felt that our parents would not approve of. In those days, we were not allowed to participate in many activities such as dances, movies, games, playing cards, or things like checkers. We spent a lot of our time reading, playing with dolls, or just playing outdoor games.

We also were never allowed to use profanity. My parents did not use it, and they tried very hard to shield us from people who did use it. Also, fighting and arguing were not allowed, and if they caught us, we were quickly reprimanded. My mother always said, "Brothers and sisters should never fight or argue with one another" or "It takes two to argue and if one of you be quiet, the other one will stop talking." Those were words of wisdom. I did not know it at the time, but I have found out that those words work in my adult life today.

> The heart of the prudent getteth knowledge and the ear of the wise seeketh knowledge. (Proverbs 18:15 KJV)

Sometimes we were teased because of my parents' strict rules. Some of the classmates called us names like "Holy Rollers," which sometimes made us feel embarrassed. But thank God, we made it through. Those same children were quick to remind us when we ever did anything that our parents would disapprove of. They would make loud comments like, "You know your daddy will get you!" The rest of the children would get a good laugh on our behalf. We really did not have a choice but to behave properly. If we did not, we knew that it was possible that it would get back to our parents. And we did not want that to happen.

I am reminded of one day, when I was about nine or ten years old. I was on the school bus headed home from school when I noticed an older student dropped a pencil when she was exiting the bus. Instead of me telling her, I picked it up and took it home with me. Later that evening while doing homework, my mother saw me with it. She questioned me on where I had received it. I told her that an older student dropped it as she was getting off the bus. I thought my mother would let me keep it, but instead she told me to take it back to the same place and drop it back down where I had picked it up. That was a hard thing for me to do, I thought, because I did not want anyone to see me dropping it for fear they would think it was mine. I did not want it to be known that I was ordered to put it there. I knew I could not take it back home. Thank God, I was able to drop it without anyone seeing me. That taught me a lesson: leave things alone if it does not belong to you.

But through it all, going to school was a lot of fun. We always rose early and caught the bus before sunrise. We were the first riders on the bus and the last ones to get off. By us living in the rural area, we had about thirty minutes to sleep on the bus before other riders got on. When school was out for the day, we returned home to do our chores and homework. Homework had to be done by nine o'clock, which was our bedtime. If homework was not finished, we often had time to do it on the bus the next morning and that we made sure of. There was no excuse to not do homework. Before my parents went home to be with the Lord, they both were blessed to see all of us attend college and seven to graduate from college. Since then, God has blessed five of us to further our education by receiving a master's degree and one received a doctorate degree. Through all this, God blessed each one to receive gainful employment and later retired in their various positions. Their jobs consist of federal government, state, education, nuclear system, oil, gas, and transportation industry in the capacity of management, law enforcement support assistant, teaching, writers, authors, supervision, engineering, commercial bus driver, drafting, and design. Many of my parents' grandchildren have also gone on to receive a college degree while others are yet pursuing a degree. Three of them have received a master's degree in various areas while one has become a lawyer. They also have been blessed to receive gainful employment. Their jobs also consist of federal government, state, business, entrepreneurship, medical and pharmaceutical industry, health care, logistics, telecommunications, barbering, real estate, oil, and gas industry. I give God all the glory.

# CHAPTER 4

# School Days and College Years

But seek you first the kingdom of
God, and his righteousness; and all
these things shall be added unto you.
—Matthew 6:33 (KJV)

*College Ambitions through Challenges*

Since I was born with medical problems, I was faced with
multiple challenges in my life. I was a very sickly child, and
my parents always had to take me to the doctor for one
problem after another. I had a speech impediment and a
mild case of cerebral palsy. I also had problem keeping up
with my peers. Regardless of my multiple doctor visits, my
parents never lost faith in God. My parents and the saints
at my church kept praying and believing God for me.

And all things, whatsoever ye shall
ask in prayer, believing, ye shall receive.
(Matthew 21:22 KJV)

When I was in the sixth grade, a special program (now called "special education") was implemented at my school. It was a pilot program to help those that were having problems keeping pace in the classroom. I believed fear kept me from being able to express myself and participate with others (I did not want others to notice my handicap, so I often kept to myself and never asked many questions). I did not want other students asking me questions about my speech or why I shook when writing.

The school administrators asked my parents if I could be a part of the special program. I thank God that they willingly agreed. I believe that was one of the best moves in my educational career. They did not permit me to wallow in my handicap, and I was always treated the same as my siblings. They kept encouraging me and made sure I was doing the best to my ability. My older siblings reinforced what my parents were doing by assisting me with extra help. In seventh grade, my life turned around. I was moved out of the special program into the regular class, and five years later, I graduated from high school.

> I can do all things through Christ
> which stengtheneth me. (Philippians 4:13
> KJV)

Upon finishing high school in 1973, my ambition was to go to college and further my education. I wanted to experience the life of living in the dormitory, but I knew my parents were limited and not financially able to pay for my college. I applied for a college loan and a college grant.

Since college was starting very soon, I moved in the dorm pending on the approval of the loan.

I was so excited about moving away from home for the first time that with my immature mind, I did not want to wait on the approval. I just thought everything was going to work in my favor. I moved my personal belongings into my dorm room, but I was only there about a week when the devastating news came. My loan had not been approved, and I needed to pay tuition or vacate the premises. That is when reality set in and my thoughts were all wrong. That was my first experience of facing a "real-life" situation concerning me. Sadly, I repacked my things and returned home. I began to pray and asked God to lead me in what to do because my desire was to attend college and further my education.

> I will instruct thee and teach thee in the way which though shalt go: I will guide thee with mine eyes. (Psalm 32:8 KJV)

After returning home, I was blessed to connect with some friends who were attending the same university. They had their own transportation, lived in my community, and were commuting to college every day. I was able to ride with them, live at home, go to school full time, and work part-time. Thank God for friends. I will never forget the kindness of those who helped me during that time. I did that for approximately two and a half years, but the stress of me working, attending school full time, and not having my own transportation took a toll on me physically. I became seriously ill.

> A man that hath friends must shew himself friendly: and there is a friend that sticketh closer than a brother. (Proverbs 18:24 KJV)

## Overcoming Obstacles

On February 22, 1976, while visiting my sister Hazel and her family, I had a traumatic experience that I had never encountered before. As I stood to walk to another room in the house, my legs became very weak and I became unbalanced. I sat down and tried to stand again, but this time I became very dizzy and there was an excruciating pain in my head. The furniture in the room seemed to be skipping about and it felt like a wrecking ball was tied around my neck, holding my head toward the floor. I could not stand without falling or get my balance. I was told by my sisters that I was screaming hysterically.

Since I was not doing any better, I was then rushed to the emergency at Ben Taub Hospital, Houston. After a long wait, I was finally examined by a doctor. He gave me some medication that helped ease the pain and told me that I needed to make an appointment to see a neurologist. A few days later, I made an appointment and was examined by a specialist. The diagnosis was "stress." He told me that I was on the verge of a nervous breakdown due to an overload of me going to school and working. He advised me to drop out of college for a while and get some needed rest. With regret, I took an emergency leave of absence for the remainder of the semester.

After resting at home for a while, my sister Sealy, who lived in Los Angeles, California, thought it might be good for me to visit her to rest and relax. After some thought, I took her up on the idea. Why not? I had never been to California. While I was there, she gave me a "crash course" in typing to help me brush up on my typing skills. After staying a couple of weeks, relaxing, and enjoying my visit, I began to feel better, both physically and mentally. As time went by, the spring semester was coming to an end and the summer was fast approaching. I returned home at the end of the semester and reentered college for the summer term. The Lord blessed me to remain in college with no problems, and I graduated two years later from Prairie View A&M University with a bachelor of arts degree, May 1978.

# CHAPTER 5

# Years of Employment

Ask, and it shall be given you;
seek, and ye shall find; knock, and
it shall be opened unto you.
—Matthew 7:7 (KJV)

*My First Job*

I started my first job when I was sixteen years old. In the town I lived in, there were very few job opportunities; on weekends I did odd jobs for people in the community, like cleaned houses, house-sat, babysat, picked peas, shelled/ snapped beans, or whatever the job might be at the time. The summer after I graduated from high school, I worked part-time doing housekeeping for different homes in the community.

As fall approached, I started college full time while I worked part-time doing housekeeping. I did that for approximately two and a half years. As I began my junior year in college, I was blessed to participate in a work study program (work on campus and attend school) on the college campus. I worked as a "student library assistant" at the W. R. Banks Library at Prairie View A&M University, where I remained until I graduated.

Whatever thy hand findeth to do, do
it with thy might. (Ecclesiastes 9:10 KJV)

### Knowing the Guidance of God

After I graduated from college, I began searching for employment. I had received a degree in art education. Those jobs were not plentiful at the time, so I decided to become a substitute teacher. I enjoyed substituting, but I needed a job with stability. I did not substitute in the summer months, so that became a huge financial burden. I was living from paycheck to paycheck and I had bills to pay; but some way God always met my needs.

During the summer, I decided to take some post-graduate courses to help enhance my résumé. On the days I was not in class, I went on various interviews, hoping and praying that a job would come my way. Then I ran into another roadblock either I did not have experience or I was overqualified. I began to pray and asked other saints to pray with me. I believed if I kept the faith, God would open the door for me. He had done it for me so many times. I had no other alternative but to trust and believe God.

And they know thy name will put their
trust in thee: for thou Lord, host not for-
saken them that seek thee. (Psalm 9:10 KJV)

I continued to substitute full time for approximately three years. I also worked on other odd jobs during the summer months. I was able to save some money, but it was never enough. It seemed like I had no place to go. It felt like my life was caving in on me, but again I remembered God. He would not put more on me than I could bear. I made up my mind that I was truly going to give God my burdens and leave them there.

> Cast thy burden upon the Lord, and
> he shall sustain thee. (Psalm 55:22 KJV)

During the summer of 1982, I began to diligently seek God like I had never done before. One day as I was lying across my bed praying and asking God for guidance, I dozed off to sleep. As I slept, I began to dream of seeing a strange cloud in the sky that was shaped like a newborn baby. As I continued to dream, I looked toward the sky; the cloud then formed into a large hand. The hand opened as if to give me something. While I was yet dreaming, I heard a voice saying, "I will pour you out a blessing that there won't be enough room to receive it." I awoke suddenly, and immediately, the scripture came to me:

> If I will not open you the windows of
> heaven, and pour you out a blessing, that
> there shall not be room enough to receive
> it. (Malachi 3:10 KJV)

Shortly after that dream, God opened the windows and provided me with a job. I became a teacher at Christian Academy School in Inglewood, California. I was interviewed and hired by telephone. In April 1983, I wrote an article in a local Christian newspaper called *The King's Messenger.* This was a personal testimony of how God provided me with that job. It reads:

## Hired by Telephone
### (A Personal Testimony)

Greeting to the saints of God everywhere. God has been good to me whereof I am thankful. During this time of economic pressures, when so many are being laid-off or fired, God is yet blessing me. I am thankful for the faith that I have to put my trust in God. Proverbs 3:5 says, "Trust in the Lord with all thine heart..."

Sometimes when it seems like you can't make it, trust God and wait on him. Psalm 27:14 says, "Wait on the Lord: be of good courage, and he shall strengthen thine heart: wait I say on the Lord". Believe that he will do what he said he would. I am a witness that God can and will. He has done it for me and he can do it for you, only trust him.

A few months ago, things began to fall apart in my life. My job was terminated, I couldn't find another one, and my bills were due. I didn't know what to do, but to trust God. Sometimes it seemed like I couldn't make it, but I believed God and he gave me the strength to go on.

One day at the end of summer, it seemed like II couldn't go any farther. That is when I raised my hands toward Heaven and said, "God, if I am going to live in this world, something is going to have to happen. I've got to receive a miracle". I meant that from the bottom of my heart. I was reminded of the scripture, "Cast thy burden upon the Lord and he shall sustain thee..." Psalm 55:22. After saying those words and completely turning my problems over to him, my burdens lifted. I began to just take one day at a time, not knowing what the future held, but I knew God held my future.

Shortly after on Tuesday, August 31, 1982, I received a telephone call informing me to call to Inglewood, California. I didn't know what to expect, but I stepped out on faith. I made that call and I believe that was one of the greatest calls that I've ever made.

It was a school that needed a teacher. I talked to one of the directors and we discussed my qualifications, experiences, etc.

I was qualified for the job, but there was one problem. They didn't know me, had no application or resume on file and they needed a teacher that following Tuesday. He let me know my chances would be slim if any, but asked me to send a resume. After hanging up I said, "God if it is your will for me to get the job and leave Houston, speak to the mans' heart. If he wants me to come, I will go."

Sure enough on Friday, September 3, 1982 I received a call from the director. She didn't really know why and this was something they did not do (interview or hire by phone), but they were going to hire me. She wanted to know was it possible for me to be at work that following Tuesday. I told her yes and began thanking God. I was blessed to get here that Monday night and today I am teaching at Christian Academy Elementary. I feel that I am blessed to be able to work with such wonderful people here at Christian Academy. They are not only concerned about the education of the child, but they are concerned about their soul.

I shall forever be grateful for this opportunity: when many were being laid-off or fired, I was hired (all was done within a week). This is why I say, "Can't nobody do me like Jesus, because He is my friend." Trust in Him and He will make a way. I am a living witness. May God continue to bless you and remember me in your prayers.

While living there, I became a member at Academy Cathedral Church, under the leadership of the late Pastor Doyle Hart. I became active with the church/school, and I enjoyed working with the staff and students. I had a lot of opportunities to meet and work with others in the community. I even had the chance to meet movie stars. I became friends with an actor who we keep in touch with until today. I also was the sixth-grade teacher to one student who later became a well-known actress and another student that does commercials. That was quite exciting for me being a country girl from a small town.

*Journey of Faith*

I lived and worked in California for about seven years when I began to get homesick. I started making preparation to return home, but I wanted to be sure that I had completed all requirements for teaching school in Texas. In February 1989, I flew home to take the TECAT (Texas Examination of Current Administration Teacher). It was a very cold and icy day. I was concerned whether I would be able to make it to the center to take the test. But by the grace of God we made it. My sister Mildred drove me to the center in that icy and cold weather. Before I got out of the car, we had a word of prayer. I walked in, believing that I was going to pass the exam. After several hours, I came out of the exam room with a big smile. I then told my sister, "I passed." A few months later, I received my results and thank God, I had successfully passed.

In July 1989, I packed up and left California in a U-Haul truck along with my brother George and my sister Sealy. My new journey of faith had begun. As we traveled back home, the concerns of not having a job was in the forefront of my mind, but I believed God was going to provide me with one. My previous experience had helped build my faith.

> So then faith cometh by hearing, and hearing by the word of God. (Romans 10:17 KJV)

As the summer ended and time for school was upon us, I still had not found employment. I went before the Lord again and said, "Here I am again, Lord. I need another blessing. I need a job." The month of August and September passed and still no job, but I had my church, family, and friends praying and believing with me. Then October 2, 1989, I received a breakthrough. I was hired on a new job. I was blessed to become a special education teacher at Smiley High School in Houston, Texas.

> Blessed are they that keep his testimonies, and that seek him with the whole heart. (Psalm 119:2 KJV)

After working at Smiley High for approximately twelve years, I decided it was time to seek for new employment at another school district. The economy was in a slump, and the cost of living continued to rise, and my salary had remained the same for three years straight. It was complicated to just maintain everyday life. I continued to pray and asked God for directions.

In 2000–2001, I began preparations to change jobs. I had not interviewed with anyone, but I began to act as though I had a job waiting for me. I began to clean and clear personal things out of my classroom as if I was moving. During the year, a few of my coworkers passed my classroom and asked, "Are you coming back next year?" With a smile on my face, I always responded by saying, "I don't plan to be here because I am praying and believing God for another job." I did not know what was in store for me, but I believed God was going to provide me with another job.

For we walk by faith, not by sight. (2 Corinthians 5:7 KJV)

In April 2001, I was asked to go on an interview in another school district. The principal was looking for a special education teacher and thank God, I was qualified. I was pleased with the interview and felt it had been successful. I was told a decision would not be made until after the school year ended. I believe God so much that I completed all the clearing and moving of my personal things out of my classroom. By the end of May, my classroom was cleaned and cleared of all my personal items.

I wrote my letter of resignation and dated it for June 20, 2001. That was the last day for resignation, and the letter had to be postdated by the 20th. I typed and kept it in my possession until I felt it was time to mail it. The school year came to an end, and I had not received a response from the principal who interviewed me. As I was talking on the phone with a friend concerning the situation, I told her that I was going to trust in God and mail my resignation letter on the next day, which was June 20.

> For everyone that asketh receiveth; and he that seeketh findeth; and to him that knocketh it shall be opened. (Matthew 7:8 KJV)

The next morning before I could mail my letter, I received a phone call from the principal that I had interviewed. She wanted to know if I was still interested in the teaching job and if I was, the job was mine. She then informed me of my duties and the paperwork that needed to be completed. When I hung up the phone, I began thanking and praising God. I became a special education teacher at Cobb Sixth Grade in the Galena Park Independent School District, Houston, Texas. I remained there for twelve years, and after thirty-one years of teaching school, I was blessed to retire in June 2013.

# CHAPTER 6

# In the Midst of Sorrow

And God shall wipe away all tears
from their eyes; and there shall be
no more death, neither sorrow.
—Revelation 21:4 (KJV)

*Death of My Father*

I was only living in Los Angeles for a few months when my dad became ill and passed. In February 1983, he suffered a massive *heart attack,* and we thought he would soon get better, but God decided differently. I was not able to be with him during his last days, but we kept a daily report of his progress. After our dad's health was not improving, my sister and I decided to make plane reservations to go home. We thought his time was short; within an hour after plane reservation was made, he had another massive *heart attack.* God called him home on February 22, 1983. It was very heartbreaking because that was the first death of someone so close to me. I did not understand why, but God gave me the strength and understanding to know that it was his will.

## *Life Is Just a Vapor*

I had an aunt who we called "Aunt Red" who lived in Los Angeles. She lived about thirty minutes from my sister and me. She was like a mother to us. We loved her dearly and was very fond of her. Whenever we got homesick for some good Southern home cooking, we visited her, and that was quite frequently. She was the only one that could cook dinner so good that it left you wanting more. But unexpectedly, that came to an end in October 1988.

It was on a beautiful Saturday evening, my sister and I decided to visit her to celebrate her seventy-fifth birthday. We offered to take her out to dinner, but instead she insisted on preparing dinner for us. Of course, she won that argument. She cooked one of our favorite meals which consisted of beef tips with gravy and mashed potatoes. No one could put together beef tips/gravy and mashed potatoes like "Aunt Red." She left us wanting more, even when there was no more. After we ate, we sat around, watched television, talked, laughed, and did some reminiscing. I had no idea that this was my last time eating and visiting with her. Finally, the time came for us to go home. We exchanged small conversations as usual, hugged one another, and I told her I would call her the following week. We always kept in touch with each other two to three times a week. We embraced one another again and departed. Little did I know what I was about to experience.

On the following Tuesday, I gave her the usual phone call, but no one answered. I thought little about it because I anticipated on calling her later or she would return my call. I went on with my daily activities, when on Thursday evening, I remembered: I had not heard from "Aunt Red." I picked up the phone and called her again, but no answer. I waited around and decided to call her back twice—still no answer. This time, I became very concerned and worried. Then I called my sister Sealy and discussed it with her. She tried to call and got the same response: "no answer." It was then that we decided to drive over to where she lived.

After arriving there, we knocked on her door, stood there and waited, but no response. We could hear the television playing through the door, yet there was silence. We began calling her name, this time more hysterically, but to no avail. Since she lived in a senior citizen apartment, we went downstairs to the main office for a key. With the help of the manager, we were finally able to enter.

After entering, we found "Aunt Red" in her bedroom slightly sitting up on her bed, with her feet crossed over one another. The television was on and her Bible was opened beside her. It looked as if she had just dozed off to sleep and never woke up. According to the coroner, she had been dead for approximately four or five days. We knew a friend that had talked to her on that Monday. It was then that I understood the true meaning of the words written in the Bible by the Epistle James.

> Whereas ye know not what shall be on the morrow. For what is your life? It is even a vapour, that appeareth for a little time, and then vanisheth away. (James 4:14 KJV)

## Delivered in a Dilemma

In April 1990, we were all saddened by the sudden death of my "uncle George." He had been my neighbor all my life. It was on a beautiful afternoon when he decided to go out and sit in his porch swing. After he was gone for so long, "Aunt Nita," his wife, went to see what he was doing. When she got outside to where he was, he was on his knees at the swing. She called his name and he did not respond. She knew something was wrong, so she immediately called for an ambulance. When they arrived, they saw that he was already dead. They told her that the coroner would be coming as soon as possible.

While waiting for the coroner to come and pronounce his death, my aunt began to call her sons and other relatives. Finally, the coroner arrived and moved his body. Other family members soon began arriving to my aunt's house and began to discuss and make final arrangements.

Meanwhile a storm began brewing in the distance. We were all sitting on my aunt's porch when the clouds began to get dark and dreary. Everybody thought it was best to go inside of the house because the weather was becoming severe. The rain began to heavily pour down and the wind began to blow furiously. It was blowing so strong and became very dark that some of us became frightened.

Suddenly, I thought I heard a train whistling in the distance, but there was no train nearby. I mentioned it to my older cousin, and he quickly motioned for me to be quiet. He did not want the younger ones to be afraid. Within minutes, the lights went out. The house shook and the backdoor of the house flew open forcefully with a "bang." Everybody began to scream hysterically. We did not know whether we were going live or die. This went on for just a few minutes, then the wind and noise calmed down.

After the storm passed, we all went outside to investigate; but it was very dark because the lights were all out. The moonlight was the only light we had. In the darkness, we could see trees had fallen in some places and mud was knee-deep. We could not see the real damage until the next morning. The storm that we witnessed the night before was a "tornado." We could clearly see the path it had taken. It came within feet of the house that my family and I was in. It went between my mother's house and my aunt's house. A tree fell on my mother's roof and damaged that, but there were no injuries. According to news reports, that tornado traveled over ten miles, demolishing everything in its path. God spared me and my family's life.

> Fear ye not therefore, ye are of more value than may sparrows. (Matthew 10:31 KJV)

*Death of My Mother*

After the death of my uncle, life began back to normalcy. I later moved to Houston to be closer to my job. While teaching at Smiley High, I had a desire to get a master's degree. I thought seriously about it and discussed it with my mother and sisters. They encouraged me and told me it could be done with the Lord's help, so I prayed and

asked God for his directions. My mother was very supportive because she knew where God had brought me. As God
started opening doors for me financially, I prepared myself
and took the appropriate test. In 1993, I entered graduated
school at Prairie View A&M University and began working
on my master's degree.

During my second semester of graduate school, my
mother became very ill and died after a brief period in
the hospital. It was a very sad time for my family and me.
We just assumed that she was going in the hospital for a
short stay as usual. We were used to her spending lengthy
times in the hospital, but this was different. We lost a true
"matriarch." She had suffered from *emphysema* for the past
few years. She was only hospitalized for three days, and on
March 2, 1994, she went home to be with the Lord.

Before she went home to be with the Lord, she wrote
a letter to her children and grandchildren. She had been
very ill over the past few years. The letter was only to be
opened at her death. The letter was written on September
11, 1986, eight years before her death. It reads,

To the Jesse & Aslee Shephard Children,

> I pray God's blessing upon each of
> you. Listen, I don't feel I will be with you
> all too long. I am asking you to be nice
> to one another. Always stay in the will of
> God. Always be somebody. I have been
> very proud of you children. Continue to
> be nice. Stay saved. Love one another. If

you have a disagreement, settle it with peace.

You all just don't know. I have been suffering quite a bit. I get up, lie down and it's still there. But through it all, I love God and I am going to continue to live for him. He has done so much for me. I thank him for it. I thank you all for being nice to me and standing by me.

I want Bob to play the sax at my funeral. Have church. You know I love lively service.

Thank my daughters-in-law and sons-in-law for what they have done for me. I don't want to be burden to you all… Study the word of God, so you will know it for yourself. Tell all my grandchildren to get saved. Tell them to read Ecclesiastes 12:1. Be somebody and don't let your friends lead you astray… I thank all of my children and I love you all.

Children, I love the Lord. He has done so much for me. But when our time is up, we have to go. I am very weak in my body. I am trying to make it… I thank God for the heartaches and pain. I don't regret the disappointments and going without… There were times when I did not have, but I praised God… You may not have everything you need or want, just keep on living for him. I know he can do it. Don't give up so easy. God got a way.

Above all of my suffering, I thank God for a saved life in Christ Jesus. One day, trouble will soon be over. I am on my way home. I know my Redeemer liveth. Stand up for holiness. Don't let nothing turn you around. Don't try to fight your own battle. Let God. It will be well fought... Please get along with one another. Thanks again for caring for me... One of my songs is "I Got A Testimony and I Am So Glad." I want to meet all of you in Heaven... May God bless each of you... I asked God to let me live until you all could do for yourselves, so he did. I thank him for that. Now I am waiting on the Lord. Love you all.

I love you all,<br>
Mother

With great sorrow, we had lost someone very dear to us. It seemed like I could not go on, but deep within I could hear the encouraging words of my mother saying, "Go ahead." With God's help, I did. I continued with the graduate program, and about a year and a half later, I graduated with a Masters of Education degree in Guidance and Counseling from Prairie View A&M University, May 1995. I know without God, I never would have made it. I learned if I trust and believe in God, there is nothing too hard for him. To God be the glory.

> Behold, I am the Lord, the God of all flesh: is there anything too hard for me? (Jeremiah 32:27 KJV)

# CHAPTER 7

# Dreams Become a Reality

Delight thyself also in the Lord; and he
shall give thee the desires of thine heart.
—Psalm 37:4 (KJV)

*Wishes Do Come True!*

As a young child, I always had a yearning to travel across the
United States. Over the years, I read many different books
that kept my interest, especially *Black American History.*
I was always interested about my ancestors and their
many struggles. Visiting the Black Museum in Baltimore,
Maryland, Little Rock Central High School in Little Rock,
Arkansas, and the Martin Luther King Center in Atlanta,
Georgia, were very educational. Knowing what my fore-
parents went through has helped me to stay focused on
where I am going. I wish every child had the opportunity
to see how blessed we are as a people to live in this country.

I also wanted to see other historical places that I had
never seen or been before. When my church offered a tour
to go to one of the Hawaiian Islands, I was excited to sign

up. In January 1984, while living in California, my church took an eight-day tour to Honolulu, Hawaii. That was one of my joyous opportunities that was given to me.

Out of all the most memorable and exciting vacations that I have taken were in Honolulu and New York. In Honolulu, Pearl Harbor was one of the most unforgettable ones. I had the chance to visit and stand where historical events took place. The opportunity to set foot on land that some regard as sacred was unimaginable. As I stood over the "USS *Arizona*" and read the names of the men who lost their lives, it sent chills down my spine. I could only visualize the fear that surrounded them. But due to their bravery, they were able to face their enemies. I could relive those moments in my subconscious mind. We must never forget those brave men and women who died protecting and serving our country.

I also visited the famous "Kodak Show," and there we saw and took pictures of the "hula dancers" performing. We proceeded to visit the different museums that gave me a better insight of the Hawaiian culture. Every Friday was a special day in which they called "Hang Loose Day." On this day, the men wore Hawaiian shirts, and the ladies wore muumuu dresses. When they spoke to you on the streets, they would give you the "hang loose" sign. This was a tradition that majority of the natives observed.

One of our last visits in Hawaii was the Pineapple Factory. There we were able to see the process of pineapples being prepared from the fields to canning, from canning to shipping, and from shipping to the dining table. Before leaving the factory, we were given a bowl of fresh pineapples to eat and enjoy. While eating them, I observed the difference in taste. The fresh pineapples were dried, crispy, bittersweet, and lacked the taste of preservatives; the canned pineapples were soft and juicy.

In New York, I had the opportunity to visit the Statue of Liberty and the Apollo Theater. At the Statue of Liberty, I was able to see and read the famous words of Emma Lazarus: "Give me your tired, your poor, your huddled masses yearning to breathe free." We also attended "Amateur Night at the Apollo," and a group of students from Smiley High School, Houston, performed and won first place. We were very excited to take back the trophy. I was a teacher at Smiley High, and I was one of the chaperones who attended the field trip.

Since then, I have been blessed to travel across the USA and one country. God has granted me many desires of my heart, and I will be forever grateful. Every trip that I have taken has been exciting, educational, rewarding, and even some spiritual like the Holy Land Experience in Orlando, Florida. The chance to visit those different landmarks and explore the culture of various places have left a lasting effect on my life. Never give up your dreams on what you can accomplish in life.

# CHAPTER 8

# Financial Blessings

It is more blessed to give than receive.
—Acts 20:35 (KJV)

*Truth Grows from Faith*

In the beginning of me teaching school, my salary was small but beneficial. I was just thankful to be employed. Whenever there was an increase, so it seemed that I barely had enough to make ends meet. At that time, I was making approximately twenty-five thousand dollars a year. I prayed and told God that I needed a financial breakthrough and I needed to make at least thirty thousand dollars a year. I just had to trust and believe God.

One day while praying, it was laid upon my heart to give more to God in tithes. In my spirit, I was led to give one hundred fifty dollars every two weeks. Even though I was not making that much, I decided to just trust God. Sometimes, I went without certain things, but I was determined to do what I believed God laid in my heart. I did this for approximately one year, but one thing I noticed: God always made a way and opened doors for me. He provided me with the finance at the right time, and he continued to meet my needs time after time.

On that following year, my salary was increased to thirty-six thousand dollars a year. I am a living proof that God answers prayers because he keeps on proving himself to me.

> And prove me now herewith, with said the Lord of host. (Malachi 3:10 KJV)

I once wrote an article in *The King's Messenger,* a Christian newspaper, in June 1981. It always encouraged me to trust in God. It reads,

### Trusting in God

Greetings to the saints of God everywhere. My heart is filled with joy, knowing that Christ is in my life. Today, many seem to be in a state of depression. The joy that once was is one. Many worry about the economy, some about the violence in society and others the high unemployment rate. Bur, whatever the case might be, I know a man that has the way out. That man is Christ Jesus and all we need to do is trust in Him. *"Trust in the Lord with all thine heart; and lean not unto thine own understanding."* Proverbs 3:5

Some might ask, what is trust? My dictionary tells me that it is faith, belief, having or putting confidence in him, as we do our legs to carry us where we want to go. We don't doubt whether we can walk. We stand up and walk. Why? Because, we believe. This is the way God wants us to be; believing that He can do any anything, but fail. He can handle any situation, no matter what the problem might be. The reason I know is because He has handled my problems. He has brought me through some dark and narrow roads. Recently, I went through something only God could carry me through. The way was very dark and dreary. But, I continued praying, hoping, and believing. Truly, I can say that God brought me out alright.

Often in the past, I worried about the next day, but I have learned to take one day at a time. As I look back over the roads from which I've come; it gives me a greater determination to go on, even when it seems like there is no way. My advice is: find a place to pray and I know God will answer prayer. No matter what obstacles might come up in life, I intend to continue to trust God. I know if I keep my hands in God's hand, I will come out victoriously.

*God Said It, I Believe It*

During the end of summer 2007, I was again faced with some financial struggles even though I was paying my tithes and offerings. I realized that sometimes we go through challenges like this, but it only makes us stronger. I continued praying and seeking for more directions from God when I was reminded of what was done in the past. If he had done it before, he could do it again. I must continue to believe and not doubt.

One late night, as I was in my bed, I was watching a Christian program when my attention was drawn to the evangelist who was speaking. He asked for the television audience to mail in $1,000.00 tithes offering to help with his ministry. As I laid there and listened, I said to myself, "I don't know this preacher, and I don't know where my money would be going." Then through my subconscious mind, I heard the words, "Invest in me. Pay tithes on what you want God to bless you within 2008." I thought about it and said to myself, "I cannot lose if I invest in God." So I decided to give 10 percent every two weeks of what I "wanted" my income to be on the next year.

> Bring ye all the tithes into the store-house, that there may be meat in my house, and prove me now herewith, saith the Lord of hosts, if I will not open you the windows of heaven, and pour you out a blessing, that there shall not be room enough to receive it. (Malachi 3:10 KJV)

I was determined to try God at his word, so in September 2007, I began to give a larger amount of tithes every two weeks at the church where I was a member. I made sure that was the first offering that I would partake in. Sometimes my finances were limited, and it was hard to meet all my needs, but I always made sure that I gave my tithes first. I kept praying, believing, and trusting God.

This went on for about a year, but in July 2008, unexpected news arrived at my doorsteps. A tumor was found on my kidney and a biopsy had to be done immediately because it looked like cancer. Major surgery would have to be done very soon. The devil tried to torment me to make me believe that God had not led me to give more tithes. More doctor visits meant more bills, but I knew what God had spoken for me to do. I could not understand why all of this was happening, but I kept giving the tithes that I promised God.

I had major surgery in September 2008 and was off work for eight weeks, and two of those weeks, I received no pay. The devil again tried to torment even more, but I kept paying my tithes, praying and believing. Sometimes it seemed like I could not make it, but I knew that I had to keep the faith. God had never let me down, and I knew his grace is sufficient.

## God's Promised Is Fulfilled

I was blessed to return to work on November 4, 2008. I began to get more strength in my body, and slowly I began to get into the regular routine. I had not received all God had promised financially for the year 2008, but I made up my mind that I was going to wait and trust him. After all of what I had gone through, I had faith that he was going to do what he promised.

> The Lord is not slack concerning his promise. (2 Peter 3:9 KJV)

The end of 2008 came and went. The devil tried to torment my mind, reminding me the year had ended and I had not gotten my financial blessing that I expected in 2008. Again, I went to God in prayer, saying, "God, I thank you and I know what you laid on my heart. You told me to invest by giving tithes on the amount of what I wanted to receive in the year 2008. Lord, I have done it and now it is in your hands. I will continue to trust and believe in you." Little did I know, God had already answered my prayers.

> And it shall come to pass, that before they call, I will answer; and whiles they are yet speaking, I will hear. (Isaiah 65:24 KJV)

I went on with my life as usual, but on January 5, 2009, I went to the mailbox to get the mail for the day. As I looked through the mail, I noticed that one letter looked like a check could be on the inside because I could see through the window of the envelope. Before I opened the letter, I stood at the mailbox and whispered a word of prayer, saying, "Thank you, Lord, for what I am about to receive."

Since I had been diagnosed with cancer, I knew that a check was due to me; but I did not know exactly how much and when I was going to receive it. I believed God for a certain financial blessing in 2008 even though it was now January 2009. As I opened it and took a quick glance, I began thanking and praising God. My attention was quickly drawn to the date on the check. The date the check was written was December 31, 2008. Immediately, I heard the words through my subconscious mind saying, "Didn't I tell you?" God does not lie. If he said it, it will come to pass.

> God is not a man, that he should lie; neither the son of man, that should repent: hath he said, and shall he not do it? Or hath he spoken, and shall he not make it good? (Numbers 23:19 KJV)

I continued to praise God, and as I began to look back over the year, the Lord had blessed me with what I had asked for. He had blessed me with over what I had anticipated for the year 2008. I am a living witness that God answers prayers. If he promised it, just believe without a doubt that it will come to pass.

> God is no respector of persons. (Acts 10:34 KJV)

As the years passed, God continues to pour out his blessings on me in so many ways. My faith in him has become much stronger. Years later, God tested my faith in him once again. There was an out-of-town evangelist who preached at my church on a Sunday morning. The Spirit of God was very powerful that morning, and the anointing was felt throughout the building. Before the evangelist ended the service, I believe he was led by God to ask those who desire to participate in making a pledge to the church. I purposed in my heart that I wanted to be a partaker. By this time, my faith had grown tremendously that I decided in my heart to pledge. I pledged, and within that year, God blessed me financially seven times than what I had pledged. I truly say God is a miracle worker. He continues to open so many financial blessings for me, even when it seems like there is no way. I am encouraged to never lose faith in God.

## Chapter 9

# Keeping the Faith

Now faith is the substance of
things hoped for, the evidence
of things not seen.
— Hebrew 11:1 (KJV)

I am truly blessed to be able to have written a memoir of short stories/testimonies of my life and others. From a very young age, I was inspired to tell others some of the miraculous things that God has performed in my life and people around me. I feel delighted to be able to share it. Since I began writing this book, I have become a stronger person, both mentally and spiritually.

I will speak of thy testimonies also
before kings and will not be ashamed.
(Psalm 119:46 KJV)

I am so thankful that my parents reared us in the nurture and admonition of God. I often wonder if I did not have the parents who were persistent in their teaching, where I would be? I am forever grateful for their guidance. They taught us the importance of education but often reminded us that without salvation, our lives would be void. They encouraged us that we should and could be successful with education and salvation, but education without salvation was worthless.

> But bring them up in the nurture and
> admonition of the Lord. (Ephesians 6:4
> KJV)

I am healed, not because of what I have done, but because of the grace of God. I know, without a shadow of a doubt, that God can bring me out of any problem or medical diagnosis that I might receive. I know that if it is his will for me to go through it, I believe that he will give me the strength. I know that if I live for him, he will take care of me. He is the one that has control of my life, and his will must be done.

> My grace is sufficient for thee: for
> my strength is made perfect in weakness.
> (2 Corinthians 12:9 KJV)

As I live in this world, I realize that I will be faced with more trials and tribulations. The various situations that I have gone through over the years have helped build faith. I do not know what the future holds for me, but one thing I do know is that God holds my future. I am determined to hold fast to his unchanging hands. I know there is nowhere else to go, so I must depend on him. My desire is to please God and to continue to trust and believe in him.

> In the world ye hall have tribulation:
> but be of good cheer; I have overcome the
> world. (St. John 16:33 KJV)

As I travel through life, I am aware that no matter what obstacles that I am faced with, God can bring me out victoriously. I am endeavored to remember to always accept God at his word. I pray that I will never forget that he does answer prayers and above all, he will keep his promise. Until God calls me home, I want to live a life where others would be encouraged to trust and live for him.

> For whatever is born of God over-
> cometh the world: and this is the victor
> that overcometh the world, even our faith.
> (1 John 5:4 KJV)

# My Prayer

God, I thank you for blessing me to write this memoir book of short stories/testimonies. I know without you, it could not have been done.

I pray that everyone who reads this book will experience one of the greatest blessings of their life. I ask you to let them know that they, too, can have even greater testimonies.

I ask you to bless those that are going through similar or even greater situations that I went through. Let them know that miraculous experiences can also happen in their lives. Let them know that you have control of their lives and all we need to do is trust and believe in you.

I ask that those who do not know you come to know you as their personal Savior. Let them come crying and asking, "What must I do to be saved?" Lord, let my life exemplify you, that others will have a desire to serve you.

Thank you for everything that you have done for me, and I will continue to testify to others about your greatness.

These are the blessings I am asking in your name. Amen.

# Memorable Events
## "Lest We Forget"

1955: Born March 7, 1955

1957: Doctors had difficulty resuscitating me after *dental surgery*

1961: Started elementary at Prairie View Training School

1962: My brother George (fourteen years old) healed of *acute arthritis*

1966: Placed in a special education (Sped.) program in sixth grade

1967: Transferred out of Sped. to regular class; Dad had *massive stroke* at the age of forty-eight; Dad discharged from hospital/rehab in November 3

1973: Graduated from Waller High School; freshman at Prairie View A&M University

1976: Dropped out of college due to illness; returned to college in the summer

1978: Graduated with a bachelor of arts degree in art education

1979: Miraculously healed of *cerebral palsy*

1980: Received the baptism of the Holy Ghost on Thanksgiving night

1982: Hired with a telephone interview/moved to Los Angeles, California

1983: Death of my father on February 22

1988: Mother healed of a compressed vertebrae; death of my aunt "Red"; Recipient of "Who's Who Among Young American Professionals"

1989: Recipient of Christian Academy Schools Exceptional Leadership Award and Principal Award; passed TECAT (Texas Examination of Current Administration Teacher); relocated to Texas and started a new teaching job in the public school

1990: Certified in special education (language/learning disabilities)

1993: Enrolled in graduate school at Prairie View A&M University

1994: Death of my mother on March 2

1995: Graduated with a master of education degree in counseling

1998: Death of brother-in-law Charles L. Piggee

1999: A *benign tumor* was removed from my neck

2000: Death of my brother-in-law James Knight

2001: Started new employment with Galena Park ISD; death of my niece Laura Shephard (age thirty)

2003: *Benign tumor* was removed from my right kidney

2007: Miraculous increase in wages; death of brother-in-law Joe Carrington

2008: I was diagnosed with renal cell carcinoma, stage 4 (kidney cancer)

2009: My sister Sealy was diagnosed with renal cell carcinoma, stage 1 (cancer)/treatment was successful; another *benign tumor* was detected on my right kidney

2012: I had major surgery for spinal stenosis with myelopathy

2013: *RCC (kidney cancer)* returned and I had three major surgeries; retired after teaching thirty-one years; death of sister-in-law Gwendolyn Shephard

2014: I was diagnosed with end-stage renal failure/I began *dialysis*. My sister, Sealy, was diagnosed again with renal cell carcinoma, but this time her right kidney was successfully removed.

2015: Recipient of Lifetime Achievement Award from Powerhouse COGIC Youth Department; diagnosed with non-Hodgkin's lymphoma, stage 4/I had chemotherapy for five months; my sister Hazel was diagnosed with double breast cancer, stage 2/she had major surgery, five months of chemotherapy, and six weeks of radiation; my brother Bob had a *cardiac arrest* and was placed in a medically induced coma and was discharged from hospital within a month; my sister Mildred had major heart surgery; sudden death of my best friend, Mosha Marshall

2016: *RCC (kidney cancer)* returned/I had major surgery; recipient of Appreciation Award from Powerhouse COGIC; my brother George was diagnosed with colon cancer, stage 2/he had major surgery and five months of chemotherapy; I was diagnosed with Breast Cancer, stage 2/I had major surgery

2017: I was diagnosed with breast cancer, stage 2, again/I had major surgery and six weeks of radiation; death of my brother-in-law Dr. Edward G. Pollard

2018: I was hospitalized for seven days of an unknown *blood infection;* my sister Sealy was diagnosed with Hodgkin's lymphoma, stage 2/she had chemotherapy for five months and later radiation; I had non-cancerous colon surgery; my brother James had three toes amputated because of diabetes.

2019: My nieces and nephews gave my siblings and I an "Appreciation Luncheon (The '9' Jewels of the Late Jesse and Aslee Shephard)." They just wanted to show their kindness and appreciation for everything that their uncles and aunts had done for them.

2020: My niece Reginya Thompson was diagnosed as having a mild stroke. God has healed her and she is once again able to perform daily activities; sudden death of my nephew Jermaine Shephard (age thirty-eight); my sister, Sealy, died after being ill for two years. Another tumor was detected on kidney (RCC). Surgery has been scheduled for a later date. I have been diagnosed with congestive heart failure (CHF) because of the past chemo and radiation. Thank God, there was no blockage found. I am yet praising God through it all. I am yet trusting God. I know that he is a healer. Recipient of Christian Academy Educator Legacy Award.

2021: Surgery was done to repair hernia and it turned out successful.

# A Special Tribute
## to Our Sister!
### Dr. Sealy Marie Shephard-Pollard

We were so excited when you moved back home. Our lives were filled with much joy and happiness upon your return. You have always been such a great "big" sister. You were our friend and loved us unconditionally. We shared joy, laughter, sorrow, and tears. You were such an inspirational to all of us. You epitomized faith, endurance, strength, determination, and perseverance. You showed us that by receiving a master's degree at the age of sixty-five and received a doctorate degree at the age of seventy-one. You had faith in me; you edited, and encouraged me to complete this book. We will never forget your generosity, love, and kindness for your family and others shown throughout the years. You had a beautiful warm infectious smile that radiated through and through. It was such a blessing to have you here with us during your season of challenged health, but it was a greater blessing to serve you. Even though you had problems speaking at the end, but one of your last audible words were, *"Thank you, God."* In spite of our sorrow and greatly missing you, we take solace in knowing that God has given you peace, free of pain and suffering. Rest easy in the arms of Jesus!

We Love You Sister,
JJ, Jimmy, George, Bob, Hazel,
Jeanette, Jean, and Globaby

# ABOUT THE AUTHOR

Barbara Jeanette Shephard, better known as Net, was born to the late Jesse and Aslee Shephard in Houston, Texas, on March 7, 1955. She is the seventh child of nine children, five sisters, and three brothers: Jessie, Sealy, James, George, Robert, Hazel, Mildred, and Gloria. She grew up in Hockley, Texas, and attended Prairie View Training and Junior High  School. She graduated from Waller High School in May 1973. Upon completion of high school, she enrolled at Prairie View A&M University and graduated with a bachelor of arts in art education in May 1978 and a master of education in guidance and counseling in May 1995.

She worked as a substitute teacher for three years at Hempstead and Houston ISD before becoming a permanent teacher at Christian Academy Elementary School in Inglewood, California. She later became a teacher at North Forest ISD (Smiley High) Houston, Texas, where she became certified in special education. After many years of teaching high school, she became a sixth-grade math/inclusion teacher at Galena Park ISD (Cobb Sixth Grade School), Houston, Texas. After thirty-one years of teaching elementary, middle, and high school, she retired in June 2013. She now resides in Humble, Texas.

Barbara is a member of Powerhouse Church of God in Christ, Houston, Texas, where Bishop Johnny A. Tates is her pastor. She was saved and filled with the Holy Ghost on Thanksgiving night 1987. She is also a six times cancer survivor within a ten-year span. She continues to testify to others of her healing.

Barbara is the recipient of several awards: Who's Who Among Young Professionals (1988), Exceptional Leadership Award (1989), Principal Award (1989), Lifetime Achievement Award (2015), Appreciation Award (2016), and Educator Legacy Award (2020).

One of Barbara's dream was to be able to write different articles and short stories. She has written articles in the past for a Christian newspaper called *The King's Messenger*. She also loved reading and proofreading people's work. During her spare time, she loves to read, write, travel with family, watch a good Christian movie, and play video games/watch sport TV with her nieces and nephews. She also loves to surf the internet and ride her bicycle.

Her mottoes are "I am a living testimony" and "always trust God in every situation that comes your way."